This work is a book base[d on...?] ll names, emails and other identifi[...] ve been changed or modified to [...]cification and or embarrassment. All consent was given by respondents and the only feelings hurt were that of the authors.

Published through Defray & Co. Inc

All rights reserved Copyright

© 2012 Defray & Co. Inc

No part of this book and research maybe reproduced in any form without permission from Defray & Co. Inc. Thank you for respecting this request from Defray & Co. Inc.

© 2012 Defray & Co. Inc

Other titles soon to be available in this series and under

Defray & Co. Inc includes:

Guy's 101

One Week in HER World

In a Series of
What the Hell is wrong with ME:

What is it about Women....? And their Emotions

Troy Defray

For the girl who couldn't catch a break...

WHAT IS IT ABOUT WOMEN...? AND THEIR EMOTIONS

'... I have an unfavourable attitude towards relationship self help books, as the people who write them are most likely single, desperate and lonely with too much time to think with way too much to say and apparently give guidance on. Everyone and anyone these days can be an agony aunt or a "pseudo new age relationship guru" as we all have opinions valid or not. But I will not sit and read an individual of minuscule personality and experience tell me how to run my life let alone how to react and act in my personal life and relationship.... people who think that they have the right to tell you what to do and how to do it and can write about it are twits of the highest degree, I mean how dare you tell me about myself and my life and relationships when you yourself are most likely single, atavistic and go through the same problems I do and others do...

Your shit stinks as much as mine and you and everyone else can give advice like everyone can take a dump.'

S.N

A PERSONAL NOTE OF FOE

In writing, researching and getting others to read this, I have been labelled crass, arrogant, obnoxious, self contradictory and been told that I throw my smart's out for all to chock on. This may be true BUT I hold no apologies for this. I would like to thank those of you who I personally asked to read my drafts and openly critic them for feedback and sound-bites. Some of your responses and critics where all disseminated in vain and at times with pure malice on your brain- I bare no forgiveness or forgetfulness of your spites as I believe I can laugh the last laugh.

CONTENTS

1. Show of hands
   - No more small talk, it's down to the wire
     - Before you continue, please take note;

2. The Emotionally Dependent Females ARE....
     - 'The Shift'
   - In The confines of a relationship
     - And then you have Leyton: The Self imposed victim
     - Sexual assault helps and is our secret power!
   - Not in a Relationship
     - Pity party over: Let's get REAL
     - The dating scene, are we shy?
     - The Booty Call receiver (From the ex!!)
     - The One's likely to get used
     - The Secret Girlfriend
     - Stalker/Ugly faze
     - Bad Friends
   - The type of partner that they go for

3. Introducing the Emotionally Co-Dependent Females
     - The subsidiaries
   - In The confines of a relationship
     - '....It's about that time'
   - Not in a Relationship
     - Dating
     - The Friends with Benefits

- The Ex
- Game Players
- The type of partner that they go for

4. Well Hello there, Emotionally Independent Females
    - Terrified to begin??
    - My Story!
    - When they are done, they are done
    - In The confines of a Relationship
        - Their partners
    - Not in a Relationship
        - The single life is better?
        - He is set to fail
        - Dumpers Dumpees
        - Hyper sexuality or just active sex lives
    - The type of partner that they go for

5. And the Mixtures are In, Introducing the…
    - The exhaustive Emotionally Co- Dependent with Hints of emotionally Dependent extracts
        - The talkers- "talk is cheap"
        - The Katie's of the world- *Confussed.com*
        - "Number… Numbers… Numbers"
        - And then you have the RUNNERS
        - His only with you for the money
        - The one's with borderline ABANDOMENT ISSUES
        - The ones who change their appearances

- Emotionally Co-DEPENDENT with a swish of Independence and crazy!!!
  - I hear what you saying but I'm not listening
  - Feel my raft
  - Queue the DRAMA
  - And then you have Whitney
  - Sex Kittens and the Freakish
  - Partners

6. *An Interruption to THE SCHEDULE*

7. *The Miscellaneous OTHERS*
   - I'm Pregnant
   - ~~The psychotic ones~~ WTF
   - And then you have
   - The Unusual Breakup Artists

8. *SO What Does THIS ALL MEAN?*
   - So what, what does all this mean? What's he trying to say? What does he know?
   - Addressing some of the general critics!!
   - Let the good times keep rolling??
   - So what did you think about all of this

9. *Whitney KNEW!*

PLEASE BE AWARE, BEFORE READING ANY FURTHER ALL NAMES, AND IDENTIFYING CHARCTERS HAVE BEEN CHANGED TO PREVENT IDENTIFICATION OR EMBARRASMENT OF ANY SORT. THE STORIES ARE REAL BUT NAMES AND OTHER IDENTIFIERS HAVE BEEN CHANGED.

1. Show of hands

Show of hands if, you have ever sat down and listened to one of your female friends, family members, or even a work colleague talk about their significant other and how bad he is; how she cannot take it and cannot stand being with him anymore, how bad he treats her, how she is done with him, and how he even cheated on her; And so on, and so on.

She claims that she is done and is ready to become single again yet;

A DAY LATER THE SUN SHINES OUT OF HIS CRACK AND SHE STAYS WITH HIM and yet a few weeks later or give it a month she starts the complaints again: *The cycle of wondrous relationships.*

But there are those women who are in the same predicaments as their counterparts who complain about their relationship and the problems at hand and act differently within the same given situation. These women experience their partners cheating on them and two seconds later they kick him out the door. Consequently, those we earlier talked about stay, complain, talk BUT stay and their cycle continues.

We all get annoyed listening to these women; sisters, cousin's, friends' colleagues constantly go on about their turbulent relationships?

We all get tired of suggesting what should be done?

We all get irritated on the eventual lack of turn around?

If you don't, I sure as hell did (and unfortunately still do).

I got tired of hearing and making suggestions to my best friend's girlfriends, I got tired of repeating the same advice suggestions and handing out tissues to snot nosed whiners and I got tired of being the "good friend" and assumed shoulder to cry on or trying to be impartial to my sisters, friends and family and friends of friends.

I got really tired really fast as **I am no agony aunt or relationship guru.** *Clearly*!

So being as I am, the charming very obnoxious person I admit to being- told one of the snot nosed females, to *'Man up and get over the guy as he was surely over her if she really looked like that when crying.'*

The thinking at this point was to be brutally honest and see where it got me and if the suggestion would do better than the cooing I had been doing previously.

The next snot nosed viper was my sister, who I told was too submissive to her boyfriend and let him get away with too much shit. She ended up not talking to me for a week!

Yep, I put my foot in it, as I usually do- and unfortunately I did not stop dishing out my dose of suggestions then.

One of my colleagues at work always told us that she was getting ready to break up with her boyfriend as she was tired of his cheating. Tired of the way he treated her and the women of his family and general family members. I told her to *'shut it and be real.'* She was forever getting ready to break up 'with his loser self', as she so liked to put it.

> Leyton, my best friend Matt's girlfriend is another of these women I have labelled snot nosed (though for some time I have had a crazy ass crush on her- it wasn't on purpose

thought at one point I was ready to start scheming like you chicks to get her. But that's over- she is too dependent and easily mind fucked). She has been with Matt for three years and in those three years he has cheated on her constantly. But this time he slipped up big and got the other woman Shai pregnant. Leyton as usual cried and complained to me about Matt and how hurt she was and how the last time he had cheated on her she had to go on a week's course of antibiotics and feminine relief crèmes.

Oh God that's nasty! Yep, if I ever had a hard on for her at anytime it was totally eradicated by those words- My status= officially limp for her.

Leyton is determined to stand by her man three years into the relationship and at least 8 different occasions- I can recall of her being cheated on and three separate occasions of antibiotic courses. So I told her *'she liked being cheated on and it was her fault that she felt the way she did'* and then gave her a pack of condoms and told her to tell him to use this the next time he wants to cheat on her.

Some years back my aunt Tarnie- from my mum's side and totally crazy, got out of a twelve year relationship after she caught her long-term boyfriend with his best friend. To put it politely he was "poking" her from the rear when Tarnie walked into the apartment they shared in California. Tarnie being Tarnie pulled out her service weapon and decided to chase her now ex and the best friend out of the apartment and into the neighbouring condominium complex 'shooting two in the air and another one directed at [her] ex's ass.' Lucky for him she missed and lucky for Tarnie she did not get caught as her ex and his best friend where too scared to report the incident as Tarnie was the police.

Every time we talk about this incident it incites laughter in my family.

See that kind of reaction I kind of understand. Not the gun part (that's Americans for you, and for the American side of my family- incidents like that are a norm for them) **but the reaction she had.** Following in the family suit my cousin- Laure Terrie and aunt Tarnie's first niece broke up with her boyfriend of two years after he told her that '[he'd] cheated on her "just the one time"'. Talking to Laura Terrie was a different experience than talking to Leyton. LT believed that if her boyfriend of two years really loved her then he wouldn't have cheated in any capacity. To LT cheating was the ultimate betrayal of his supposed love for her so she decided to push him down the stairs which resulted in a dislocated right arm and broken left leg for him.

> → Poetic justice much? This actually makes me question the women in my family's sanity as my mum once told me that she had slipped two Viagra pills into her ex's coffee once after an argument which led him to the ER thinking his penus was defective due to his constant hard on. She laughed so hard she was crying well telling me this. My sister Anel broke her ex's nose then broke up with him after he threaten to take out a restraining order on her (though I still haven't heard the full story to that as from what I can garner she actually cheated on him and started stalking him).
> Though their reactions maybe flawed to say the least I respect the fact that they *understood their worth* and reacted than complain and stay docile as other women do that are in similar or the same situation as they were.

John Jay also known as 'lady-killer' (he gave himself that name, though no one calls him that) went out with a girl for 9 months. Within those 9 months he treated his girl like a fool, cheating and what's-not's. When she finally wised up **after 9 months of all the nonsense... she left him**. Though it took nine months and several 'what do you think and what should I do' conversations, **she finally reacted and moved on unlike Leyton**.

Four different women in very similar positions and in semi similar dysfunctional relationships yet they acted and reacted very differently. LT broke it off after her boyfriend cheated and sent him on his way battered and injured, it took Lady-killer's ex 9 months to finally gain some semblance of sense and well Leyton is still sticking in there for the long run. Now I ask:

What is it that makes these women respond differently than others (women) in the same given situation?

The answer: Emotions

Emotions are what make them act and respond differently within the same given situation in any relationship they are in. They are what give rise to a woman's reaction such as leaving her cheating partner (consequences implied) or staying and sticking it out with him.

It should be understood that not all women are emotionally inclined as others. Some women are more emotionally dependent than others; they rely and depend on their emotional ties with others. They can only feel needed or wanted when in a relationship of any sort, meaning that rather than using common sense at times needed within the relationship they are more reliant on what the "heart says".

Tram 29 one of my many interviewees and survey respondents' you will come across in this read is a prime example of an emotionally dependent female who has stayed in a relationship with a partner who for 18 months even after he had cheated on her twice and both those times she had contracted gonorrhoea and Chlamydia from him. Tram is no Ogre, she is pretty, around 5ft 6inches and obviously takes good care of herself and her body is banging. Talking to her I can't help but constantly glance at her soft full lips and fantasize about what they would taste like (or what havoc they could do to my person). Any man would kill to be with her (not only for the way she looks but she seems genuinely nice to talk to) yet she still stays with an unappreciative fool who cheats on her (and at times is verbally abusive) and obviously doesn't understand how lucky he is to be with her. Tram seems to believe that she can change him and stop his cheating ways so she sticks it out as 'he will get tired of stepping out on me one day or another and I will be there and ready for what is next for us... I know he loves me as he tells me that all the time- he just has a weakness (anger and low tolerance) that he will soon overcome.'

> Okay Tram- each to their own. **I am not here at any point to give advice,** all I want to know is what makes you think that in the year and six month you have been with him and he has obviously been cheating, will make him think otherwise to stop when you obviously encourage him to go out and seek others comfort (stop giving excuses for his behaviour and actions). If Whitney (my nut of a girlfriend) allowed me to cheat I would never want to stop.

But one piece of suggestion to all: **Set boundaries at the start of a relationship and not long after you have encouraged and allowed such behaviours or unusual norms to persist as they will be hard to change or stopped.**

Aside from Tram and the other women of her type (emotionally dependent); other women can be independent of their emotions within the context of a relationship. These women, unlike Leyton and Tram are not easy push over's or easily manipulated- *they gives as good as they get and can handle their own in every sense*, and would act completely the opposite when in the same situation as the emotionally dependent female(s).

***J**essica 34 from North Carolina stated on her survey that she broke up with her partner through an email that she sent to all their friends and family and CC'd the 'bitch he decided to cheat on me with.... I wanted them all to know that he was a cheating bastard who was screwing about on me while I was pregnant with our son. After I kicked him out of our house I sent his things to him with added presents inside (a couple dead mice, a few stinking fish tails and whatever was able to make his things smell like crap and ruin them). I didn't put that tidbit of information in my law suit against him for emotional misconduct and abuse while heavily pregnant.'*

***P**aula 28 said, 'I tell my friends who bitch and complain about their other half to get over it and shut up. If you have a problem then sort it and don't stay there complaining and bitching to me as that does nothing than raise your blood pressure and **annoy the hell out of me**. When my friends come complaining I tell them that all the time as I really do not care to get into your* *mess. My husband and I have our problems and so do millions of other couples but what I do not stand for is any disrespect and he knows this. I would leave him at the drop of a hat if he disrespected me in any way that is beyond repair, and he knows this- love or no love I will not put up with his bullshit.'*

***

Relationships and women are the two most puzzling things for me and most other men in this world. I constantly get asked on advice for relationship problems and issues. My answers always vary as it really depends on your partner and what the actual situation(s) and or issue(s) are. But recently I have noticed that the questions are what to do when blah happen(s)? Or why does *she* act like this and what should I do?

My answer to those individuals are- *'To be honest I am not sure, but let's talk about it and see if we can find the real problem.'*

You see I detest openly giving advice on individual's relationship and girlfriend and boyfriend issues- that's not me or what I do as I find people DO NOT like to adhere to advice given (**And personally way too many people feel qualified to dish out unwarranted and unnecessary personalized advice- and look at my track record on advice giving!**). Those who seek the advice yet deviate from what is said and thoughts handed out waste my time for which I am always seeking to recover those wasted minutes and seconds that others have wasted.

My experiences have led me to the conclusion that the messenger is always shot as no one likes to hear the truth as *'what does he know, he is a man for one and two... he don't know me and what I be dealing with.'*

BUT YET, YOU SORT ME OUT FOR THE ADVICE TWIT!

Do not seek what you are truly not ready for.

For that, I do not openly advertise that I am a PhD student studying psychology, or that I work for a crisis centre that deals with "ALL" matters of crisis and intervention at **work places, institutions and wherever we are needed and contracted out to and not anything to do with personal relationships**. Telling anyone this or allowing my profession to be known has made me a target for the (whinny voice implied) 'can you help me... What should I do when...? What do you think about this? Am I crazy?'

> → *Btw to the last question asked: If you have to ask then most likely you are!*

As of a week ago I stopped handing out personal suggestions (as I so love to call them- sarcasm implied) to those who came to me in need. If you are not paying me for my skills you are not getting my words. The last person I imparted some personal suggestions to was Leyton after she had found out that Matt had cheated on her again and was expecting.

Leyton is what I like to call a serial victim. She is a self appointed victim due to her dependency of her relationships and her unwillingness to remove herself from situations that are not beneficial for herself such as her relationship with Matt. The condom suggestion was one of many, after anything went wrong or crazy between them, I would be called and made to play "the shoulder" by Leyton, then she would call Matt or he would call her and then presto they were good. Matt cheated gave her STI's and I advised her to take time off their relationship and do her- *she took it as stay with Matt and let him take me to dinner and away for the weekend to apologize for his silly mistake.*

SERIOUSLY- SILLY MISTAKE! OKAY

I give up where they are concerned- all sayings fall on deaf ears when it comes to them and many others. *I buy extra condoms and give him so he can protect himself and Leyton, but it seems bareback and reckless is his thing.*

In better words, let us move on and we can later discuss the workings of such dysfunctional relationships.

- **No more small talk, it's down to the wire now**

'Is she crazy? She emailed a picture of me naked to everyone including my boss! It wasn't funny when I had to explain and lie that my email account got hacked by my now ex girlfriend and HR got involved.'- Toby 29

That's funny; this outtake is one of many along these same lines. I have heard these statements and such questions many times from guys and women (who are the more likely perpetrator of such acts). Sometimes it's not just emailing naked pictures of their ex or partners, its posting what the guy gave them such as Lani did:

Lani 27 stated, my ex cheated on me and I found out when I went for a check-up as I was having discomfort down there. I found out that the bastard gave me a dose of thrush and genital warts so I thought it just to make any and everyone aware of what he came with. I created a FB page dedicated to him with a posted picture of him and by the side of the picture was another picture of what herpes looked like with a caption of; 'this is what you get when you get involved with this trash'- add me. Hahahahahha, I sent requests to everyone on his page and mine which included some of his work friends, family and our friends. Just in case they did not check their FB on a regular basis I text the same picture and caption to his phone list.

Lani you are dangerous, but creative at that.

So instead of giving situational advice, where I would ask 'what would you do in such and if such, how do you feel' and so on, I decided to ask questions to the public using interviews via my website, public forums, street surveys and other such ways to get a more wide and varied answer. I even questioned my next door neighbour and individuals who I met on my trips abroad on the plane to see their reactions to many of these same situations that many women and guys go through. These situations where in reference to that of the ones we discussed above with the examples of Leyton, LT, my aunt Tarnie and others. Having my question in hand, I gathered enough information using my research background to formulate a hypothesis (boring talk for assumption making) to aide me formulate a reasonable explanation to that of my answer to my question posed earlier (on why women respond differently within the same given situation) to get a more concrete and conclusive ending.

I reiterate this read is no self help book or 'know how' manuscript; it's more of a discussion of many minds which pokes fun invariantly (using real case studies and real examples) at the different reactions to the same one situation. To make haste so that we can begin our analogue of discussion, explanation and general piss taking I declare that in my search for an answer I came across one of many finding which is that there are three types of emotional states a woman can present within some sort of romantic or sexual relationship. These emotional states dictate the nature and balance in the relationship and can help us answer the question of: *Why some women react differently when in the same given situation.* These emotional states when observed many times present distinct characteristics. Characteristics, that defines the individuals and how they react within given circumstances in relationships. (These circumstances relate to break ups, arguments, cheating partners and other situations that can arise and would trigger some sort of reaction within a relationship.)

So, what are these emotional states? Well here we go:

> **Emotionally Dependant Females:** Submissive to a 'T', you tend to be very dependant of being in that relationship regardless of its true nature. **You feed off being in that relationship or relationships period**. You tend to go with the flow of the relationship as you believe that things may right themselves soon... Or you have the notion of: *'He treats me nice and what is there out there?'* (More than what you are actually getting now)
>
> These relationships tend to be destructive and last longer than standard relationships with very negative and abusive outcomes. Unfortunately these are common relationship states for a significant proportion of the female population.

Example: Ava 42 says, 'relationships are not easy and sometimes I can do and say the wrong thing's which makes my partner react in ways. We have had physical altercations' and verbal assaults, the police have been involved before and I have walked around with black eyes and a busted lip but am down for my man as I can take what I get from him as I put it out there. I am not embarrassed about telling you this as I love my man and can't imagine what I would do if we were not together or if he was to leave me. '

Emotionally Co Dependant Females: These women are the true middle of both groups. You are neither dependent nor independent as you're always unsure of 'what will happen next'. **You play cautious and are neither submissive by nature but at times show tendencies of submissiveness.** You tend to show some emotional independence though you are more likely to emotionally invest in relationships as that significant other is always "the one". Oh and did I mention that you have the belief in the existence of "THE ONE". <u>You're the type that listens to slow jams straight after a break up or fight and prioritizes the lyrics as having a significant importance to your emotional state.</u>

Janey 34 says, 'When my husband asked me to marry him- I wrote the pros and cons of being with him for however long. I weighed my options and the fact that I wanted to get married before I turned 30 so that I could be a youngish hippest mum. I wanted to be a MILF which if I may- I am now. My love for him was a small factor in my list and our crazy sex life was a large pro.'

Emotionally Independent Females: These women are the most independent females, **independent of their emotions and emotional states**. They are class 'A' opportunistic- *'Can I take his penis to go?'*
They are the women with the most type 'A' male personality who are likely to be commitment fobs' and hook-up (booty call) bunnies. They are the straight talkers of the entire bunch and can be viewed as emotionally aggressive, with tendencies to be bullish.

Terrance 28 stated, 'My ex dumped me two weeks before my birthday and our 5th anniversary and told me that she was seeing someone else with something more than I could offer her. She's a bitch. A blood sucking bitch who I thought I was ready to settle down with. Her new boyfriend apparently is some sort of big shot contractor with endless funds. Money hungry bitch!'

Maggie 31, 'I have way too many what If's in life and past relationships. I think at times I react too hastily without thinking of the consequences, how I really feel, and how to word what I am trying to express during heated situations. I broke up with my ex after a stupid argument, and left it too late for us to reconcile. When I was ready he'd already started dating someone new. She's now his fiancée- that could have been me.

- **Before you continue, please take note;**

At no point will I be disclaiming that all women are different as we all rightly know they are. Everything written came from extensive observations at first that lent note to my more inquisitive and always searching for an answer nature on personal relations: Especially those relations recounted by women in regards to their circumstances, feelings and experiences. Some of the categories mentioned have subsidiaries which will be discussed further in-depth, though we will only be focusing on the more common subsidiaries found and the types of women likely to exhibit these three emotions. The three categories to an extent highlight the kind of guys these women are likely to go for and possibly attract. For example, Emotionally Independent females tend to go for bullshitless men. They like men that know what they want in life though at times hard to find so they go for the first guy who may present to them- no issues or drama and 'know where we stand at all times' type of partner.

Megan 33, 'If you are not on my level- pay check, bank account, occupation and living arrangement then you needs to step aside. I had this one guy that was still living at home (with his mother) at the age of 35 and says that he is a comic book sales man. What the hell is a comic book sales man, can anyone tell me? I told him to walk along, and keep walking- don't look back. I know at times I can come across like a ball buster but I have my best interests at heart.'

2. The Emotionally Dependent Females ARE...

There are certain women who rely on the existence of romantic/ intimate relationships. To these women, the romantic/ intimate relationship has a higher rank of importance than natural relationships such as parent-child, and friend to friend relationships. Therefore, due to the higher rank of importance of these relationships these women become OVER invested emotionally and physically in these relationships.

The relationship becomes their life and they become dependent on the relationship lasting.

Women such as these are naturally needy of a relationship and clingy in the relationship- *wonder what Freud would say about them!*

As the relationship develops their attachment to their partner becomes ten times stronger (and more unreasonable) than that of a normal intimate relationship attachment. The relationships tend to be unhealthy due to the over attachment and dependency of the woman on **being with that partner in that relationship**.

So who are these females!

I introduced you to a few earlier which included Leyton, but as it is my nature to define for better understanding, I give you a working definition of an *emotionally dependent female*.

The dictionary defines the word Dependent, as 'someone who is very reliant on another'. Emotionally dependent females are no different. These women are very dependent on being in a relationship regardless of the true nature of the relationship. These relationships may be as destructive as an atomic bomb or as nurturing as a mother to a new born baby. Their core belief is that there is nothing else out there. The relationships for this group of women may lack the love, lust and or sexual desire of relationship within the other categories. These women tend to lack a reasonable length of time between relationships.

As this definition highlights, emotionally dependent females are basically needy in all sense. Without the confines of the relationship she has nothing; the relationship maybe the pits but at least she has the relationship: A relationship that has one of the most dysfunctional balances within the relationships.

The balance essentially is the power play between the couple. Basically, who holds the cards or who runs the show! As these women are emotionally dependent, their partners hold the cards at all times. Therefore, the balance goes from being of semi equal basis (as no relationship is totally equal) to one partner (not the emotionally dependent female) taking on a more leadership/dictatorial stance. This transfer of balance is called 'The Shift'.

- **'The Shift'**

The Shift simply is the unconscious transfer of power play from being a 'balanced' entity within the realm of the relationship to a more one-sided play. Example:

Leanne 27 stated that she had tried the injection (contraception) two years ago; when she initially had it, she became blotted, constantly spotted and had problems with her time of the month- so she stopped getting the injection and went back on the pill. Leanne started dating Simon a year back. He told her to take the injection as he didn't like using a condom and that he thought she would be forgetful with the pill. Leanne knowing what the injection did to her went back onto it (suffering the same symptoms as before) as Simon was too "persuasive" she said.

The shift within the relationship can happen either at the initial start of the relationship (Leanne) or can happen as a gradual process (also known as progressive shift). If the shift happens at the initial start of the relationship, it is because the guy or partner finds it easy to manipulate the woman and due to lack of boundaries at the start of the relationship formation. If the shift occurs as a gradual process it is within a long-term relationship, typically a marriage.

The women in this situation, bit by bit allow their partners extensive freedom in what is expected in the relationship. *'I have to ask permission from Simon when I want to go out with friends, on holidays and sometimes to visit family.'-Leanne 27*

Instead, the initial full on education of the do's and don'ts at the start of the relationship is absent: Thereby creating a skew of absentmindedness of his part.

In short, these women do not speak up when something is wrong or when needed. They allow for a code of silence when he doesn't call you back the same day after his missed your call. They allow him to get away with talking out of terms to your parents. They say nothing when he shows them contempt or lack of respect. They complain to friends (such as Leyton does to me) and family.

It is safe to say that these females are the least respected females of any of the categories as **they are viewed as weak and non responsive. They are more likely to back down and stay in the shadows than step out of line. Their partners are always the dominant ones. Their relationships last for unreasonable lengths of time.** And they endure more than needed for the sake of that relationship. They are *the quiet sufferers* but the bravest of any of the groups.

I say this as a way of contradicting myself and challenging my real despite for women of this category. These women endure more than most, as they are the ones that put themselves in these situations and are the ones that find it the hardest to come out from such situations.

These females are the likely victims of the missionary position; they are sexually submissive and unfulfilled. They go with the flow than interject and make their partners feel like they are inept.

Alice 40 is what we like to call a relationship junkie:

Total length of time between relationships- 1 day to a full month; Total length of time in any relationship- as long as can be regardless of the situation.
Alice's motto, "we can make this work, I will change baby, am sorry." (I use a Mr. T accent to make it sound funny)

Alice has been in troubled relationships and now in a seemingly 'decent' relationship with her current long term boyfriend, who proposed to her then, took the ring back after an argument. Her boyfriend has cheated several times and even fathered a child with an ex best friend and Alice continues to stay with him as she loves him and will deal with the issues as they come: "His worth it".

Simon 30, an attorney and his wife a 29 year old administrator have been together since high school. He openly admits to have an overly domineering attitude with regards to his and his wife's relationship. In fact he says that that's his character in all situations and he aims not to change it regardless. He wears the pants in the house and lets his wife know this. He describes his wife as way-laid, very submissive and shirks away from any type of problem by nature.
Simon states;

'She has no choice and she knows it, she listens to what I say and how I say to do stuff as she knows no better. I have broken up with her several times over the years as I didn't want to buy her a Christmas present, birthday present or even an anniversary present. She still took me back, so I thought why not marry her. Her best friend told her that I had made a pass at her and some other shit (which I had) so I told her that her best friend was a bad influence and not to talk to her again if she wanted to be with me. We don't see the best friend anymore unless it's an occasion she happens to be at.'

Montana 32, of Eastern European descent openly admits being in relationships way past the time needed to be in it. She has been in very abusive relationships and finds it hard to know when enough is enough.

Montana states-

'I love too hard; it's my drug of choice. I have been with my current guy for about three crazy years. He is crazy, but I am not ready to quit him yet!'

Shandra 31, has had an on and off again relationship with Toby for the last 9 years. It has been on and off again due to Toby's constant cheating behaviour. They have a six year old son together, but this has not stopped Toby's behaviour or changed the nature of their relationship.

Lilly 38, is too worried to start trying to correct her boyfriends actions now as they have been going out far too long and she doesn't want there to be any unnecessary problems which might lead to them breaking up as their relationship is too fragile.

Tasha 25 doesn't feel that she can get her husband to stop disrespecting her and her family. She hasn't talked to him about it before and doesn't know how to broach the subject with him now. As she does not know how he will take it or what will happen if she does.

In all, these women have relationships that are most likely to have a very unbalanced dynamic than any of the others groups yet to be discussed where one partner is more dominant over the other. Therefore the emotional dependent females can be very repressive by nature whereas the dominate partner is suppressive as shown by Montana, Shandra and the others.

- **In The confines of a relationship**

Family who? Friends? 'I don't understand who or what these words are!'

You drop your friends and family quick time for that guy/partner. It may not be intentional but with you ladies it's eventually done as you develop the notion that those people are holding you back in your relationship. It's sad as you believe that these relations are keeping you from giving your partner your all and everything.

We get it, you love him, he's 'your life' but for how long ladies?

You have heard me using the term relationship junkies in relation to the emotionally dependent women that is because they are junkies of the relationship form: They are in love with the idea of being in a relationship, the idea or feeling of being in 'love', 'needed', and even 'wanted'.

To give you a better idea of such dynamics, think of the films: *Sleeping with the Enemy* or *what's Love Got to Do with it* where you have the male antagonist characters, and the silent passive yet 'strong' wife figures. Before each wife breaks free of their husbands, the relationship is very off balanced. You have the lead antagonists as the 'be all and know all' in both the women's worlds.

Sam 40 a labourer, admits to telling his wife how to dress, how to act and what not to do, he makes no attempt to change this behaviour as he likes things 'my way'.

'If I don't like what she's wearing or doing I tell her and she doesn't argue with me or my reasoning. She once met me at work for lunch and I thought the skirt she was wearing was inappropriate, so I told her to go home and change. She did- no arguments at all.'

→ Simon meet Sam, Sam meet Simon- what utter twats!!

Nicole 29 an Art teacher from North London has been with her boyfriend for 4 years. Nicole says that like most relationships,

'John and I have had our fair share of arguments.' And rather than argue with John at times, she agrees and allows him to get his way as, *'I could do without the argument or problems that can arise.'*

Emerald 34 says, '... I have found the solution in maintaining long lasting relationships.' Answer- 'Let him get his way, it makes life easier.'

Natalie 55 was married to Stephen for ten years but they had been together for 5 years prior to getting married. Within those fifteen years, Natalie states that Stephen always reminded her of her short comings and how unworthy she was of him. Stephen would tell her of what she couldn't do and how great his ex girlfriend (who had dumped him before he had gotten together with Natalie) was; how his ex was the only one who got him off after three licks. How she was the only woman who bought him the right clothes and did everything perfect. Natalie says that they didn't have the most perfect relationship but she loved Stephen- faults and all- and would have stayed with him regardless. Stephen left Natalie a few months back by moving all his stuff out one weekend when she was out of town. When she returned back home, she found divorce papers left by Stephen on their bed. He had moved in with his ex.

Sam, Nicole, Emerald and Natalie have somewhat representative relationships of emotional dependents, though you may feel like I have chosen the extreme and negative end of this group.

So without further a 'do:

Let us discuss the positives of emotional dependents. They have longer lasting relationships than any of the other groups. These women can teach the emotional Independents about sustainability. Seriously!

They learn to deal with their partners over time thereby understanding them and really knowing them: Knowing what to do and how to act after an argument, or a blowout.

- **And then you have Leyton:** *The Self imposed Victim*

You heard me earlier mention Leyton- *my best friend* Matt's girlfriend and their highly dysfunctional and ever drama infused relationship. Having been together for around three years, Matt has tripped from one affair to the next while Leyton stayed idly by his side dealing with the consequences.

Is this what a "ride or die" chick is?

After Matt's last indiscretion with Shai and the news of a possible baby and Leyton's lack- of- there reaction I decided it was time I understood more on their relationship and most importantly *why Leyton was so hell bent on allowing such liberties and disrespect occur by*

Matt indirectly and directly to her with nothing done to try and stop such actions from Matt.

Talking to Leyton is another story, moving past my lust for her, she is a well educated and spoken female with the most ridiculous thought processes when it comes to Matt. *'I know he cheats on me and I still stay with him, I can't explain it. I love him... My last boyfriend prior to Matt was different, he treated me like a Queen, and when we broke up after he had a drunken one night stand I left him as I couldn't take it. But yet Matt has cheated on me ex amount of times and am still here crying and complaining to you. You must think I have issues!'*

'You have major issues- serious ones!'

'Troy no one likes a dick, stop acting like one.'

'How is it you can sit here and talk to me so, yet when it comes to Matt you act like a shy school girl? *Can I ask you something, why are you okay with him cheating on you, why do you let him get away with it?'*

'That was two questions, not one.' She smiles and shrugs her shoulders, *'I don't know. I say love but I don't know. I think it's more that I'm afraid to lose him more than I allow his cheating. Does that make sense?'*

'No, I don't get that reasoning at all.'

'You're really going to act like a prick through this or should we just talk when you stop acting like you're on your period?'

'Leyton, I'm trying here. I'm sorry if you feel that I'm acting like a prick, but you said you *broke up with your ex for cheating on you once while being drunk, but Matt hasn't been drunk all those times his cheated on you,* so *No,* I don't understand whatever reasoning you put behind it, or whichever way you try and justify it.'

'You're the one who brought up this subject and asked me about why I am still with Matt, and now your acting judgmental. I will take his cheating over not being with him as I love him. Blame love and my stubbornness to be with him. Call or say what you want about me- I don't care!'

'Well there we have it; you love Matt enough to be with him regardless of the cheating. So what do you want his baby to call you? Mum, step mum or the woman screwing my dad?'

'Fuck you'

'I was outer line but Ley, see it this way: you where in a relationship with a guy who messed up once and cut him loose, and now you are with a guy who makes it his mission goal to continually mess up every time he can more than the last and you call me a prick? He is my best friend and you're my friend who I care for. It's a shame he carries on like this- but like I have said to him- *you deserve better.'*

'He is a great guy, and I love him because of that- Faults and all. I blame those bitches who put themselves out there for him as enticement, it's not his fault if he is enticed- I would be too.'

'I take it back- you are not as smart as I thought and said you where! I have to go, you're killing me.'

Talking to a brick wall much?

- ***Sexual assault helps and is our secret power!***

→ **Content advisory as the next few pages contain cases with explicit and sexual details. For those with sensitive minds and eyes or those with food in their mouths be aware**

In one of the first interviews I conducted, I met Linda a 43 year old PA. She was hilarity all the way and thoroughly shocking- (*said in my best English Uppity accent*)

Linda 43, I suck his dick that shuts him up and stops the argument from escalating. I know I'm not going to win and it would just get worse so I get on my knees and go at him from the floor. Sometimes I even dress up in his favourite nurses outfit, cook him his favourite for dinner and gives him an "oral bath" (dick sucking) then all is good.

> My mouth gapped at this point, I bit my bottom lip and blinked twice.
>
> 'Thank you Linda... But I don't think that was the question, I mean the answer... I don't know what the question was again!'

I have to admit that after talking to Linda I went home and attempted to argue with Whitney, as why not- maybe an oral bath would be in store for me! *Right?* Well no! Whit told me to spin on it once I told her to give me an "oral bath" and cook my dinner just wearing an apron so that I wouldn't get any angrier.

I didn't get an oral for a week, and well dinner- I ate humble pie. So heads up guys- *don't try it at home.* And Linda like I said before- your man is lucky.

It seems the other women of this section had the same kind of thought process when it came to the question of *"how they dealt with their partners after an argument."*

Tanya 28 has been with Nana 29 for about eight years. 'After we argue Nana is all for giving me an anal exercise. It's his way of teaching me a lesson!'

Mel 20, 'I give him a hand job while he drives as an apology so that he can stop being mad at me.'

Vince 33 says that 'after a fight with his wife is the best time to further manipulate her. Especially as it's the only time his wife would willingly go swinging with him and not kick up a fuss.'

Lara says that she cooks Johnny a roast dinner then he pops a Viagra pill, before they have sex, she takes out her dentures gives him an oral as "he really likes it". She puts on her leather thongs as "it's his favourite."

'That's 20 minutes of bliss for him and well twenty minutes where his not pissed with me.'

Interesting!

- **Not in a Relationship**

    How to start? Easy, rip the band aide off quick:

    You remember those friends and family that you where so quick to dump once you started seeing him?

    Yeah those one, well ladies it's funny how fast you remember them and reinsert them back in your lives as they are 'my best friend and that's my fam- only ones there for me...'

    They now are allowed to exist and mix in your world- As "who else do I have!"

Delilah, 'Once my cousin broke up with her ex, we were allowed back into her life. We were negative influences in her relationship when they were together but now they are over- or should I say as he dumped her as he said that 'she was too fat for him and having sex with her felt like having sex with a underinflated bouncy castle' she remembered us. I give her hell about that as bitch should remember who will always be there for her- FAT OR NOT.'

- **Pity party over: Let's get REAL**

    These women are as fragile after and during a break up like a new born baby's immune system to the unknown viruses. These women are the most susceptible to be screwed over by a potential new suitor. When I say screwed over, I mean imagine some humiliation and some.

    So in true fashion let's discuss these incidents further by breaking them up into events.

- **The dating scene, are we shy?**

    Not really regulars on the dating scene as they are relationship junkies. So they tend to be the shy, easily intimidated and come off weird.

Sally 36 wrote;

My friend thought it would be funny to get me back into the dating world by making me go to a "mixer"; I got so nervous that I threw up in the toilets and smelt like stale milk all night. I didn't get any numbers.

Nigelic 45 stated- I felt so out of place going speed dating with a group of other single ladies from work. I remember talking to some guy I thought was nice about how much I love carrots. He just kept staring at me so I kept waffling on

Nancy 28, 'it wasn't that bad. I think if I would have opened up a bit more and maybe have talked then I would have gotten a number or two. I just felt out of sort. I didn't feel comfortable speed dating.

Meggy 34- 'My sister just got out of a long and hostile relationship and I thought it would be a great idea for her to get out there... It was so funny watching my sister trip over every word she would say. I set my sister up on a double date blind date- with me, my boyfriend and his cousin. I don't know if it was nerves, or what but she called or insinuated that my boyfriend's cousin was fat and single because he was fat, and may possibly be a retard. It was funny. He got so red faced and puffy- he officially hates my sister.'

- **The Booty Call receiver. (From the ex!!)**

    You are more likely TO BE the booty-call: Therefore, YOU RECEIVE **(NOT MAKE)** THE CALL.

    He calls you in the middle of the night, drunk or sober telling you to *'come over, I miss you babe.'*

    → **Let's not front- YOU WILL GO and this is a STUPID move.** This is why:

It is because that booty call is most likely your ex who's just horny and wanting a quickie: Nothing more nothing less.

<**HE JUST WANTS SEX**; HE DOESN'T WANT TO RECONNECT, FIX OR TALK ABOUT YOUR RELATIONSHIP as in his mind it's done. HE **JUST WANTS SEX**- *Primal animalistic sex*>

So what do you ladies do? Become delusional and **Do this:**

1. You get giddy and excited that his contacted you
2. You call a friend or two to mould and imply what you believe that he is saying with regards to that call. Most likely you'd have told your friend that *'his called me and said he misses me and wants to sort things out between us.'*
3. As previously stated; *you go and you guys have sex*. But before the sex, he is all 'sweet and loving' when you get there **HOWEVER,** once the sex is over- he turns around and says something like, '... Hun, *shut the door on your way out and thanks again for tonight.'*

→ **Fingers crossed: He may even give you a quick kiss to show his appreciation.**

4. *You*: Get to his house and expect to talk everything out, he ravishes you on site. So you wait and think that after the sex you're going to finally 'talk'. That doesn't happen as his kicked you out after having sex. You're hurt and pissed that 'you fell for that'.

<Dumbass comes to mind.>

5. Heads up Ladies this is not the end. Your ex will do this again and again before you finally realize. He, will booty call you and you're more likely to keep responding *'as you never know, this time might be the time. He still loves me- I know this.'*

Serena 28 wrote; 'My ex broke up with me over a year ago. But we are still sleeping with each other. He still calls me and I figure that we will get back together soon as he obviously still loves and wants me: His probably just going through something like a midlife crisis.'

Sam 33, '... The ex and I still hook up now and again. I have no problem with it as I still love him and I am finding it hard to move on. I think his seeing someone new though.'

Janet 40 said;

'After 16 years of marriage I have become his bed bunny. I am too old to be dating or out on the market. Who would want to be single at this age? I will take what his giving me so that at least I don't sleep alone.'

Gemma 30 said;

I was my ex's booty call for six months after we broke up. I thought we would get back together. But he wasn't interested in getting back together. He moved on and stopped cold calling me for sex in the middle of the day. I still miss him.'

- ### The One's likely to get used

    Ladies, so you start seeing someone new. And knowing you, you develop strong feelings for him quick. You ignore the obvious signs and his constant demands and wants from you. He is in all essences using you for sex and most importantly MONEY but your common sense is too eroded to see through this.

    Ladies, the fact that this *someone* uses you as their personal ATM goes unnoticed to you till it's too late: At first it starts off as a backhanded favour- 'babe get me something to eat', then soon leading to him asking you to give him some pocket change such as £20 as 'I'm kinda skint and I'll pay you back soon, promise babe.'

    It then escalates to him asking you for more money as, '…. You wouldn't believe what just happened…. So can I borrow a few hundred's from you babe, promise I'll pay you back.'

    You really wouldn't believe how many times this happens!

@Ladyannonymous stated;

My ex owes me a total of $6,000. We had broken up and where still seeing each other. Well, actually it was more like him calling me when he wanted to hook up or needed something more from me. I got sucked in and ended up given him a good chunk of my life savings as he needed the money to get his car which had apparently impounded. We are still on and off and he still hasn't paid up. He tells me that his working on giving me the money back every time I ask.

@HisexyZoe#36

'I was seeing this guy on and off for a while. I really liked him so, when he would ask me for money I thought it was no problem. I would always be broke and when I would ask him for the money back he always had a ready excuse. I thought nothing of it. But, when I looked at my bank statements to see where I could improve on my expenses- as I hated being broke, I noticed that I had given this guy close to £800 just in the space of three months. That had to stop. I asked for the money back and to this day I have received not a penny to the sum.'

Jill 24; 'I was a personal banker to my ex Shawn. All he seemed to want from me was sex and money. It took me $2,340 and a few broken friendships to realize this.'

- **The Secret Girlfriend**

    Ohhh, the secret girlfriend- this is how it goes;

    You front and pretending that:

    'He really does like me,'

'We are seeing each other but 'WE' (**really he**) are not labelling what we have together.'

'His not trying to hide our relationship status or hide the fact that I am with him by saying his single or pretending that nothing is going on between us. He just doesn't like too many people in our business. He's a private person.'

Pull another one!

@SimpleSimonSays

'I once "dated" this girl at school for some months. Really we just hooked up, no real dating at all. I was with someone and told her that 'we had to keep it quiet as I was breaking up with my girl'. The break up never happened and I kept sleeping with her till I dumped her. None of my friends knew till recently when I told my best friend about hooking up with his brothers now girlfriend. LOL'

Nate 29 wrote;

I am sleeping with one of my co-workers!

It just happened after a group of us from work went for drinks. I got plastered and she gave me a ride home. I invited her up and well things happened. She thought it meant something, I told her yeah- 'It means I had to get wasted to sleep with you'. She told everyone we were a couple, fortunately for me no one believed her as they thought I was still with my ex. I still hook up with her while I seek out Mrs. Right. She definitely is my secret bang- I would die if anyone knew we were hooking up.'

Ladies if he is hiding you then it's because he doesn't want anyone to know he is with you let alone screwing the 'shit outta you.'

Evarichmond31@******.com stated

I was in a secret relationship for two years till I finally got the message. **He didn't want to be seen with me.** *We were just friends to others and in private he was my boyfriend.* ***I never met his friends or family and we never really went out on date dates.***

Lance 34 wrote;

…. She liked me and would do anything to get with me so I made her 'my girlfriend behind closed doors'. I do like her but I love being seen as a free agent to other women.

How I see it is that the more desperate these women are in getting with you the more likely that they won't care in what capacity they get added to your life.

Desperate is a harsh word though rightly used where these women are concerned.

Actually, desperate....?

Nah,

But, stupid *yes*- In not seeing what was before their eyes. Eva he went out with you for 2 years, 2 years without an actual date? Two years without meeting a single friend. *I mean seriously.*

Bells should have been sounding when he wouldn't introduce you to anyone or even take you out for a nice meal. Harsh words but Eva you were a fool for that one. I am hoping you learnt from this.

- **Stalker/Ugly faze**

   'What's his Facebook status say?'

   'Who was that he was talking to and why was she all over him?'

   'Should I call him, and ask him about her?'

   'I'm gonna call him and see what he thought he was playing at bringing her to the club.'

Leslie 23

'I would call my ex crying, asking him why he was punishing me. Didn't he know how much I loved him and what I would do for him? This went on for about a week till he disconnected his number. None of his friends would give me his new number.'

@KrystalClear25,

My ex took his new girlfriend to our club. It's where we first met. I walked up to him and asked him what he was playing at... Then called his girlfriends a home wrecking cunt and slapped her. I cringe now I think about it.

Terry 35,

I would go through my ex Facebook page. When I would see a picture of a girl on it I would call him up demanding who it is. I would write a comment under her picture- calling her hoe or something crazy. He de-friended me.

@Juniormassive 29 stated;

I went to a friend's bbq with my girl when my ex whom I'd recently broken up with, came hurling at me. She was screaming and shouting about; '... You bastard, you're doing this on purpose, embarrassing me by bringing this hussy to our friends house in front of all our friends.' She attacked my girl- pulling her hair and trying to rip off her clothes. It took four of us to get her off my girl. Now who was being crazy?

- ## Bad Friends

    Ladies fronting pretending and being generally delusional are common grounds for you. **You want to believe in the impossible of that relationship. You want to believe that he will come back to you, that he will love you like you**

deserve to be. But what you don't get is that you don't exude the confidence in distilling this in him. *Over years you have let him treat you so-so and now you think he will know your worth?*

So why do you think that he will come running back?

Friends you do not help.

BE real with your emotionally dependent friends.

DO NOT encourage her with all of the above thinking.

DO NOT get her drunk and allow her near a phone or telecommunications device as she will call him endless times begging him to 'please take me back', or Facebook him with random embarrassing messages. Which will lead him to de-friending her and changing his number.

BE there for her, and ALLOW her to get really over him. FIND fun activities that will get her mind off the ex and that will allow her grow from that.

Lilly****@gmail.com said;

'I became good friends with my brothers ex when they were together, so when he dumped her I took her paintballing so that she could relieve the stress and I confiscated her cell as drunk dialling is a bitch. And my brother is a bigger dick.'

***

Leyton when you are ready to see sense, I will be there as a friend and make sure you get the help you need. Matt I will continue to buy extra packets of protection to give to you. Hopefully they will create the injection for men soon and I will supply him with a life time's supply of it. I snigger as I write this.

Personally, am not a fan of the emotional dependents, but I have to give them props, they are a tenacious bunch. What they lack in self worth and common sense they make up in how relentless they are.

They have lower partner counts and not as sexually promiscuous- meaning that you could probably count the number of partners that they have had of one hand. They don't sleep about much when out of a relationship; they tend to lean to one guy/ partner or none at all.

So, in the case of the 'booty call' that they may receive will be the only person that they are likely to sleep with.

But with all groups or some groups you have your radical extremists. And in terms of the emotional dependents you have those with low inhibition, low self esteem, and low self worth with impeded moral values.

These women are desperate for the 'relationship factor' and will sleep around to fill the void of being lonely.

- **The type of partner that they go for**

    After reading this chapter, you see the pattern that develops with who these women go for. Their partners are the total opposites of them.

    They tend to be overbearing, arrogant, and full of the sense of entitlement- *aka Matt*.

3. Introducing The Emotionally Co-Dependent Females

I have been trying to think up some sort of comedic or witty way to start up this next section but I can't think of any. So I decided that I would profess my respect for these women and move on to discussing them in greater depth.

@Remi#WTF

I am not crazy, nor am I easily intimidated. I am the kind of girlfriend who doesn't mind her boyfriend going out with a few friends which also may include a hot chick. My boyfriend has a co-worker that's a stunner and she is single. I am by no means threatened by her though she has legs that reach the skies and beautiful brown skin and has the kind of smartness that I could only dream of. He says I have nothing to worry about and I believe him and trust him enough to turn on his phones GPS system and track his movements. I love my apple! Though I trust him implicitly that doesn't mean that I would have no qualms when he went on holiday with a few of his friends and co-workers- which obviously included her SO I rearranged my work schedule to allow me go as well. I trust him but I don't trust the both of them together in the Dominican Republic.'

> @Remi#WTF, I reached the conclusion that your boyfriend already hit that and keeps hitting the sexy co-worker as I know others that would (including myself though I like to think that I am not that kind of guy) regardless of what they say.

In true fashion as the previous chapter I have decided to follow suite and define the Emotionally Co- Dependents as to give you a clearer picture of this group of women.

The emotionally co-dependent female are a common features of Chick flicks, romance books and any book featuring some sort of female lead. These women are the most agreeable group for most men. They are the Lara Croft's with a more arrogant subtlety. They are the most malleable and easy going females. They can sure as hell hang with the guys but know when to 'fall back' and allow their partners to breath. Realistically they can be viewed as the true middle ground female, though their co-dependence means that they can be moderately swayed one way or the other depending on the situation. They are essentially Co-Dependent as they have more dependent emotions that outweigh your independent emotions.

This definition allows for the interpretation that Emotionally Co- Dependent females are the most rational thinkers of any of the three categories. *This in comparison is rightly so.* The Emotional Co-Dependents know and understand when *'he is no good for me'*; **they understand what healthy relationships are about**, (unlike the emotional dependents). They don't mind working towards bettering their relationships without giving up when they face problems (look at the Emotionally Independent females).

These women understand how to make the best out of a bad situation- They can essentially work with what they've got.

Simone 23

I wasn't going to stand there while he treated me and our son like we meant nothing to him. He would choose when he wanted to be a father, which was a rarity so I made the decision for him and kicked him out of both our lives. My son doesn't need a father who doesn't want to be a father 100% of the time, he needs stability and I give him that.

Tracy M, 46 says

'My husband and I decided after 17 years of being married, to have a more open relationship. I think it's great, it took him a while and a few threats to leave him to get around the idea but now his for it. After 17 years of having sex with my husband I can now officially cheat and it won't be considered cheating.'

Audrey 27 stated 'I had been married two years before my husband first cheated on me. It was tough dealing with it, but we eventually over came it. Till three years later when I found out that he was sleeping with my sister's best friend. What's that saying; fool me once shame on you, fool me twice shame on me? I'm in the process of divorcing him and taking the house I don't blame her neither do I blame him so much as I blame myself for not listening to those that said "once a cheater always a cheater."'

@TraciAnngonkillhim.net, 'I got dumped by my fiancé or should I say left at the altar during the wedding ceremony. Am guessing he couldn't handle the 'till death us do part', so he split. He left me weeping on my wedding day and called me the next day acting like nothing happened... It took me time but now at least I can talk about it without breaking down or wanting him dead... Though I was almost tempted to put out a contract on his life but I was too scared to do so seen as there are a lot of women getting caught by the police doing such things.'

During this interview with @TraciAnn, the one question that came to mind after she told me her story was- *'Have you seen him since that happened, and what was your reaction?'* I had to ask as I know plenty of women who would ripe him a new one and bury him remains their front porch. (Mainly those women are Aunt Tarnie and most likely Anel who broke her ex's nose)

@TraciAnngonkillhim.net, '.... Unfortunately yeah, when he finally came to get his things from the garage where I had put it all. I had this vision or fantasy of getting him back by seducing him and then leaving him chained up naked to a bed somewhere. But he wasn't worth the thought of planning any sort of revenge. It was nearly 4 months later and I was too emotionally raw to be bothered with his sorry self.'

Angela 32 stated;

'I did a background check on an ex when we started getting serious. Turns out, his middle name is Savage (I liked that). He had lived in Melbourne, Germany, and Kenya and had visited France and California a few times over the year, (which I felt made him very cultured and sexy). Oh and he had three kids by three different women from the places that he had lived or visited. I wasn't ready to be baby mama no.4, so I bolted.'

> This group of female are great at philosophizing: 'He may not be the greatest guy but I can work with him as I love him.'

Lauren 30 'He [Tony, her boyfriend] may be an arse at times but I love him and wouldn't change a thing about him ever.'

Charlotte A wrote; 'Brian my fiancé is such a nerd. He is clumsy, very smart and so thoughtful. He even bumbled the proposal but I thought it was sweet- at that point I definitely knew I wanted to spend my life with him. It was a definite YES!'

Tara 54

'For the last twenty years I have been married to Mark... He does this thing after sex which I used to find funny. Now, I can't stand it. But what can I do about it, it's his thing but it's not bad enough for me to leave him. It's just smelly.'

'What's this 'thing' you found funny and smelly? I asked.

Tara, 'He would fart when it was time for him to "finish". It was funny and made him adorable, but as time went on the farts started to really irritate me- I got him to go see someone about it.'

'Is he fixed?' *It was the only natural question to ask after she said that!*

'No, but it means that he gets less sex from me. Just smelling the farts while am about to finish or still in the mood is a game changer... But his thing has helped us because he's too embarrassed of it which means that he won't cheat or think of cheating anytime soon. That's one thing I don't have to worry about.'

- **The subsidiaries**

    A large proportion of females would presumably identify themselves as emotionally co-dependent. As right as these women believe they are, though, they technically are wrong. The reason to this is that the Emotionally Co-Dependent group exists as two mixtures named as one.

    You ask- what the hell is he on about? **Well This:**

Within the emotionally co-dependent group there are subsidiaries which are the Emotionally Co-Dependent Dependents and the Emotionally Co-Dependent Independent's (Chapter 5). These two subsidiaries share many similarities that it is better understood as one- the Emotional Co-Dependents.

To better understand here are some classic examples of these the subsidiaries that makes up the Emotional Co-Dependent females:

Lee 30 'My son's father is back in our lives. He left me while I was pregnant with him and now two years later wants us to get back together. I think am going to give him a try- I'm still in love with him.'- Emotional Co-Dependent Dependent.

Ama*****@yahoo.com wrote;

'I got so pissed (drunk) one night when I went out with the girls that my boyfriend and I ended up having an argument. I ended up locking him in the bathroom all night as he pissed me off. The next morning I forgot where I threw the keys to unlock the bathroom so I left him in there and went to my mum's to use the bathroom.' - Emotional Co-Dependent Independent.

Angelic Sue 40 said;

'When I first got with my husband I hated his dog so much that I had it put down: He still thinks it ran away. I did feel bad till I

remembered it ruined my favourite bra.'- Emotional Co-Dependent Independent.

@LaurelTBC.net, 'I once burned my husband's sports jersey after an argument. It felt good and his face was a picture, at the time. But then I felt bad after and got him tickets to the game and a new jersey.' - Emotional Co-Dependent Dependent.

Angelic your different, my girlfriend Whitney would probably like you and you her. She once fed me dog food after I commented on how bad I thought her mother's cooking was. She laughed as she told me what she did- *worried much? I think so.*

It was also the last time I was stupid enough to express how bad her mother's cooking was. She once made lasagne- well I think it was. I had the shit's just looking at it and after eating it, she has never admitted to messing with that but I think she did.

Whitney is definitely an Emotional Co-Dependent Independent. I say this as they (Emotional Co-Dependent Independents) can be a tad neurotic which strangely, is a turn- on for me. (Chapter 5)

- **In The confines of a relationship**

    Now getting back to the Emotionally Co- Dependents as a whole and their experiences within a relationship

→ Your theme song: Single ladies; Put a Ring On it- *'...Because if he loves me as he claims he would never want to lose me to another man.'- @nattiedre4eva*

→ Favourite film: Anything where the woman kicks a bit of arse- Lara Croft as she's the female Indiana Jones.

Sometimes seemingly boring within relationships; Emotional Co Dependents are dependent on their relationship but **understand** how to cope when they are not around. This is in the sense of making relationship changes and decisions.

These females learnt the art of compromising a long time ago. They understand that in a relationship it's all about give and take.

'...Everyone is equal so do not act like your above the law as I am the Law! - Tarnie

The Emotionally Co-Dependent females **are masters** of their partner(s) (unlike the emotionally dependent females).

These women believe that they are the true equals of their partners.

If there was a ribbon or an award for game playing these women would win it hands down. They can run rings around their partners. They invented and co wrote the manual on ***Game Playing 101: How to get him barking***

like a dog and whimpering after you. Unlike the Emotionally Independents females, the Co-Dependents' are patient and this is what makes them expert game players.

Warning: Partners of these women **BE AWARE** you have the sneakiest opponents on the spectrum of a game you may not know you are playing.

In an interesting yet, I don't know conversation with ***Lara an accounting executive,*** who had this to say about the topic of "game playing"

'So I wanted to get anal bleaching done- as I thought it would be a great look and something to spice up things between me and the hubby. Plus, I heard that it heightens the sensation when having anal or being rimmed. I f I told my husband how much it would cost he would say NO. So I decided that I wouldn't tell him the truth and would guilty trip him into paying the amount needed.'

My response: 'Anal bleaching, Googling it right now.'

Lara- 'A few days before I decided on how I was going to get the money from him, I was really nice to him. He didn't have to beg me for an oral as always. One night I swear I sucked him off for close to 20 minutes. I even let him follow through.'

'He must have been really happy by that?'

Lara, 'I finally decided that I would do the easiest thing and trick him in thinking that he had forgotten one of our anniversaries. (He always nearly did, plus I would make up new ones when needed). That day I remember him coming home and I started shouting at him to get the fuck out of the house till remembered our anniversary that he had missed.

I would have chucked something at him for the more dramatic effect if I could deal with the clean up after my supposed anger.'

She laughs, and then says;

'I think he wasn't in the mood or not interested in me having a tantrum as he gave me the credit card and told me to enjoy. I got the anal bleaching done; unfortunately I didn't notice anything sexually spectacular with it. Though, we have more anal now than we did before. Maybe it turns him on more that it looks as it does now.'

I have no follow-up to that, other than I learned a new thing- *anal bleaching!*

Next!

Traya B, 39

'Easiest way to get what I want is to threaten to leave him or tell his mum that he got a tattoo: He maybe a 40 year old man but his still a mummy's boy who hates to get her angry.'

Holly 29

'Anytime I want something or want my way, I give him an oral. It works all the time as he knows how much I hate sucking on his penis. It looks and tastes weird.'

> Do men really cave in when some sort of sexual act on them by a woman is performed? Are we really that easily manipulated by an oral as a significant number of respondents seemed to imply that through their experiences!

Harry 45

'My wife doesn't think I know this but when she wants me to clean something like the grill- which I really hate, or go to some sort of event with her- she allows me get frisky with her in the back seat parked up somewhere. These are the only times we lets me act out our teenage years. I will take that anytime if it means going to a boring functions or event.'

Nigel 43 laughs at Harry and says

'You have it good… Anytime Melissa (his wife) wants me to do anything she knows I will say no to. She won't cook or have sex with me till I cave in. It happens a lot so at times I'm walking around with a constant hard on.'

Andrew 31, 'My wife cries. It's annoying and really irritates me as she sounds like Whales singing. That's not pretty by the way; I sometimes get it confused with her laugh. She wanted us to go on a double date with her parents. I told her that was weird. And well the sound started coming out. I swear it sounded like I had hooked her up to the home entertainment system.'

Sarah 22, 'I get my boyfriend real hard and when I know his about to burst I stop whatever am doing as if he wants us to finish then he will do whatever I say- like teach me to drive. It's either let me have my way or walk around with blue balls.'

Liz 28, 'Game playing is my forte as its fun to mind fuck and not be the recipient of the mind fuck. I feel like it keeps our love motivated. My boyfriend thinks it makes me a freak and him a freak for liking my game playing. I don't see any harm in game playing, it's actually the opposite.'

@GAGALOVER21, 'Game playing is not a bad thing for us women to do. As we do it to keeps things alive in our relationships and makes a relationship interesting at all times'

- ***'.... It's about that time'***

Ever heard the phrase- *"beating a dead horse"*

These women can tell when it's time to stop 'beating a dead horse' when it's time to move on; *You have tried 'training' your boyfriend, husband, partner for God knows how long and they still don't get it.* Now, unlike the emotional dependents (and the Independents who do not bother at times to try), the co-dependent females at least though they may not get anywhere or may have slightly improved their partners they persistently try as "he may finally get it".

Maxine 50 said, 'I have been an eternal girlfriend for twenty four years and only upgraded to a fiancé a year ago. I stopped talking as the more I talk the more time and air I waste. Maybe by my 80th birthday I will have at least upgraded to being a wife. There is always hope.'

Lisa 39 stated; 'I learnt that leaving hints for birthday and anniversary presents work. He finally got it that he sucks at gifts. For our first anniversary when we were just a couple, he bought me a "How to make the perfect origami set"; I thought it was a joke when I took it out of its wrapping- just to see his face and knew that it wasn't. My birthday and anniversary presents from him for the following years were a mixture of Applebee's gift cards, gas station flowers and monogrammed handkerchief. Who still uses handkerchiefs'?'

>Lisa I do!! They beat using countless amounts of "harsh for the nose" tissues!

Rena 24

'My boyfriend loves having drunk sloppy sex after a night out. I can't stand it, but he loves it. So sometimes when I know his coming back home drunk, I lock him out of the bedroom. The sex is always better when his sober, I don't know why he doesn't get it.'

Linda 48

'I stopped my husband from going down on me once I turned 40. After he would get done, it would feel like I had been given a paprika bath by his tongue. I told him that now we are moving into the most comfortable era of our marriage he didn't need to do it anymore as I hated it.'

Richie 55 wrote;

I find that my husband only gets things when an outsider says it. I talk to him constantly about his weight and he never does anything about it. The kids and the family have also talked to him about it and he doesn't seem to take it in. He feels like we are trying to take the piss out of him. We aren't, we just want him to know that we care about him and don't want anything to happen to him.

We went out of town a few months back and happened to bump into an old family friend, who straightway commented on my husband's size. He made a few comments which seemed to strike home with my husband. When we got back to town, within a few days he got a personal trainer and nutritionist. One talk from an outsider had him running to the gym, while years of talking and complaining about his weight did shit all.

- **Not in a Relationship**

   They philosophize:

   'If it's meant to be then it will'

   'You have to kiss your frogs till you get your prince'

   'Not all relationships are meant to last'

   'He was such a tool, am better off single'

   'Single and ready to mingle'

- **Dating**

   These women do the date scene. They get that some dates go good and some really bad; THEY ARE THE WOMEN WITH THE BACK UP PLANS FOR BAD DATES. They will always let you know where your date is headed to and if there will be other possible dates.

Michael%^&%@dbl.com wrote;*

I couldn't believe it when she told me that she 'had no underwear on and was ready for me to take her home.' I was like- 'This is my kind of chick.' We went back to her place as I wasn't going to take her back to mine as you never know what kind of crazy she may be if she is offering it straight after a 30 min date. I left her place while she was asleep; I grabbed my stuff and ran out quick.

@IambetterthanTonyHawks stated;

'I went on a date with this chick I met on Craigslist. Within 10 minutes of our date, she got up told me that 'this wasn't going to work out' then walked out. Never heard from her again! Was it something I said?'

Adam 24; 'I tried to hook up my brother with one of my work friends he really liked. Whatever was said between them or done- I don't know, as she used her Facebook to blast him then blocked me on Facebook and took me off blackberry ping- she stopped talking to me. I wonder what was so bad!'

- **The Friends with Benefits**

    These women have friends with benefits, not fuck buddies as *'that's too crude and they are friends with benefits. Thank you very much!''*

'I may not be in relationships but a woman has needs and I am a woman with needs that need to be satisfied. So what if I am not with someone!'

Their 'friends with benefit' companion actually is more likely to be a friend of some sort. **An ex maybe, but this is unlikely as when these women break up with their ex's it's more finally with no going back' (emotional dependents).** These women understand that *only under slim chances do 'friends with benefits' develop into something more-* they are realistic and not idealistic.

@SexyBrandie23 stated;

I have been hooking up with my best friend for a little while now. His only recently become my best friend since we started sleeping together as I feel like I can talk to him more and he understands. We didn't really discuss doing it, nor did we actually like each other much like that. It just happened one night and since then. We don't want much from each other- just the occasional hook up.

Evelyn***@whosthedaddy.net stated;

I once had a "friends with benefit" with my roommates. It was four of us sharing a house during university as we hated the dorms. We would regularly sleep together, no gay stuff though. It was fun while it lasted.

Annette 33, 'I think it's actually healthy. Everyone should at least have a "friend with benefit"' as I find it's better than masturbating with no company. Self Service is not all that fun as you seen it on the telly... Hehehe'

Irene P,

'I started sleeping with my roommate- who is also my ex. It's not messy but fun. He walked in on me doing a little 'finger jockey' on my own one night and asked if he could join in. It's made us closer but there is no way that we would get back together. We just love sleeping together.'

- **The Ex**

**Newly single Emotional Co-Dependents this part applies to you. **

>**The deal is**: 'How do I get him (the ex) mad jealous. As I want him to understand that this is what he fucked up being with' <all hand motions and attitude implied>
>
>**Your Solution**: Except for the night(s) out with the girls celebrating your freedom from "that bastard". You ladies are likely to date someone that you know would 'wind the bleep' out of your ex's. It's your last act of 'F U' towards him.

Rena A 20 says;

'... I got with his brother. I felt no way about it as I have always fancied his brother more than him and he knew it. I did the walk of shame the next morning and said Hi to him on my way out. His facial expressional = PRICELESS.'

- **Game Players**

    Even being single does not stop these women. Remember they are big time game players regardless. The game playing is their ammo.

    'The "hard to get card" keeps him guessing if am interested.'

    So what do you do?

Nancy 22

'... Oh I have this rule- Never pick up his call straight away. Let the call ring at least 3 to 4 times before you pick up. Sometimes miss a few calls it makes them crazy mad. Or wait even better, call him, when he doesn't pick up I call myself or get one of my girls to keep calling me so that when he calls he gets the "call waiting" sign- makes him think that I have another guy blowing up my phone.'

Li 38 said, *'I let things escalate slowly- can't give him all the goods straight away. It's all about sexual teasing- blue balls and all. Every time we meet up, I allow him one step closer to my "gates of heaven". Each time he thinks he's going to get closer.'*

Li, you are what we guys call a 'Cock-Tease'. No one likes a cock tease.

QueenAbby$%^&&@6544.com 29 wrote; 'It's all about getting the most use of him, so on the first or so date- I show him that am interested by allowing him go down on me. That way I moan and groan- make him feel like his king by just doing that. I can make myself squirt on point so he feels like his actually made it happen: Keeps him there till I find a good use for him. LOL'

Samantha 40, 'I always act like my schedule is crazy busy so they don't think that am waiting on their calls. You never want to look eager'

June 28 said,

'I do the thing where I pretend to 'accidentally' butt dial his number. Or my butt sends him an incoherent text so that he responds.'

'Do people still do that?' I ask

June laughs and responds, *'All the time.'*

- **The type of partner that they go for**

    For the other groups (Emotionally Dependents and Independents) the phrase- 'opposites attract' would best suit a description of their types of partners. But for this group, the more similar their partners are to them the likely the partnership.

4. Well Hello there, Emotionally Independent Females

Vicki******@yahoo.com wrote;

'I have no shame and nothing to be embarrassed for. I am who I am due to my experiences and my past- **NO I AM NOT JADED** *nor do I feel dislike or disdain for the opposite sex and how I treat some of the guys I have been with. I do you as you do me.'*

'When we broke up, I told my ex that he was just a **sperm donor** *and not to get his hopes caught up in being anything more than I allowed in our child's life.' I was eight months pregnant when our relationship fell apart. I was hurt but couldn't get too caught up in that feeling or the emotions that where bombarding my body and mind at the time as it was not healthy or beneficial to me. - @ballbusterismyname.net*

Welcome to the lives and thought's of the Emotionally Independent few- the ones that are likely classified **"BALLBUSTERS",** to put in nicer terms.

The most independent, opportunistic manipulative women: These women know what they want and how to get it. They can go to great lengths for what they want, but they don't want to: it's all about the short cuts in life for them.

These women are dominant ALPHA type females that are considered aggressive with bull- like tactics. They have bullish attitudes towards the females of the other categories as they view these women as **weak, inferior** AND **placid** to themselves. Their relationships **DO NOT** last longer than needed: She accomplishes and gets all that is needed and wanted out of that relationship before moving on. She is a strong believer in the hook-up system; **she sets the guidelines and rules of any relationship**. She is the ultimate relationship control freak- the total opposite of their respective partner(s).

Danny's 32 say's her motto is: **'If I call you pick up, as its for one thing only- Sex.'**

Wilma 41- 'I like to set boundaries with whoever I am seeing. He needs to understand that I'm not like most women- **I won't take his shit**, I was never made to be that patient.'

Dee 26- 'I don't like for him [her boyfriend] to leave any of his stuff at my house. I like you, maybe love you, BUT I love my space without your clutter in it. I tell him that all the time.'

Bridgett 29- 'I have this pet peeve that I hate and which my boyfriend seems to love to do- **He loves to cuddle and hug after sex, I tell him** that I have an early start and that I think it's time for him **to leave**. I'm a bitch to him but he runs back all the time.

I mean you're all sweaty after sex, why do you want to hug. It's nasty and sweaty.

Treat them mean right?'

Lysett 30- 'I dumped my ex as he couldn't give me an orgasm: Even orally. If, I'm with you and my vibrator does a better job than you do...? Then [he has] to go!'

- **Terrified to begin??**

    Where to start with this group of women!

    Emotionally Independent more like EMOTIONALLY WRECKLESS B***HES.

    Yes I said it, (*as I bet you are all thinking it*) I don't hate on them though!

    I love women and wave the flag for feminism but seriously women unlike men can go that extra mile to make a man truly feel worthless- and well these women can do a great job of it. I personally feel that **these women should walk around with a warning and hazard sign so that potential partners are aware.**

    I will admit this one time and one time only: I once dated one of these women who used me and made a mockery of my feeling for her.

    Years later and Yes I admit that I am still smarting from her, my pride and ego are still frayed. She messed me up bad and destroyed for a time (and maybe still now) my belief system in women and their rationality.

- **My Story!** *(I maybe pissy about this but it's only right- seen as I can talk about others I should be able to divulge my own experience(s))*

If I come off embittered- you may well understand why.

(This section will be removed from **my copy and hard drive** as Whitney, my sisters and family would laugh at this and me- they probably would love Mrs. Xxxx after this... plus it's way too embarrassing **BUT** I dedicate this part to the woman who humiliated me and was another untold catalyst for me in this project.)

She emasculated me for a little while- that's what Regina my colleague at work said when I told her what happened. *-Must have been drunk or stupid to have told Regina as she spread the whole ordeal to the other members in our department which lead my manager to question if 'I was really okay and if I needed counselling?'* (Yes I cocked my brows straight into my hair line when he came out with that. Regina is another bitch as she fits rightly in this group! That was the last time I opened up about my personal life near or around Regina.)

***

A few years back, before I started seeing Whit, I went to this bar to celebrate with a few of the guys on one of their engagements. Matt, his brother John, (the biggest twat I know- yes it runs in their family) JJ- aka lady-killer (serial cheater with the girlfriend issue) and some of our other friends. We had all been drinking, catching up and generally having a good time. I was doing my thing and not really paying attention to any of the ladies (as I was trying to do the single life thing since I was a bachelor again).

Within an hour of us being there, in walks Xxxxx (yes I have decided not to give her a name after the shit she pulled and the fact that I am still bitter from her stunt that she doesn't deserve to be named). Xxxxx was stunning, tall athletic build, curves in all the right places with creamy dark caramel skin and dark chocolate eyes.

Anyways enough describing you get my gist: *She was a stunner and had that short-crop Halle Berry thing going on with her hair.*

She was ordering drinks for herself and some friends (who I never got to meet) when I pretended to bump into her while trying to do something or another. I apologized and bought her a drink to apologize and from there we started talking. She seemed really cool and down to earth: Beautiful, smart well dressed with what seemed like a laid back attitude- what more could I ask for. We talked for about an hour till the guys came looking for me. I introduced them to her and she joined us. She left her friends and just hung with us like one of the guys celebrating.

When we were all leaving that night, we swapped numbers. **She called me the next day and asked me out,** we arranged to meet up that night and I took her to a fairly nice secluded restaurant in Leicester Square. We got to talking about what we both did for a living (of course I lied and told her that I was a journalist as that seemed cooler than telling her that I was a nerd and behaviourist) and what we liked and didn't like: Who our favourite super hero's were, favourite football teams and so on. We went back to hers that night and the sex was out of this world. Next day I called her and sent her a text but she didn't get *back to me right away. She didn't respond till 9pm the next day and said that she had had a crazy day, and that I should "come over". So I did.*

For a month while we were seeing each other- which was basically her calling me in the middle of the night for sex- she would never call me back or text me back when I contacted her. (Yes- I was the booty call receiver) She would decline my date offers and had at hand excuses why she couldn't meet me or call me back. We would argue about that and she would tell me 'she's sorry and would work on it.' She would come over and we would "make up" and then the next day the same issues would continue.

She would never stay the night at mine and when I raised that issue she would say, 'Tomorrow or the next time I will stay, but not tonight as I have to be up early tomorrow!' The next day or time, she would wait till I fell asleep then sneak out.

I really liked her and when I told her that she would change the subject quick time. She never talked about her ex's or anything truly personal about her.

I fell for her big time, she was smart and had a great job (which reminds me, I never got to see where she worked as she never allowed me meet her there nor did she really talk about her job. She just wore suits and dressed really nicely... hmmm interesting). She could hang with the guys, the sex was great and though things where iffy and she was a bit controlling, I liked.

Did I mention the sex was great! Who doesn't want a woman who gives them great sex regardless of everything else?

Any-who, a few months into (her indirect) arrangement of just sexing I thought it, was time for us to definitely define the relationship. I wanted the talk, so I cooked dinner and took it over to her house one night as a surprise. I knocked on the door and a half naked man opened the door. (It felt like a scene straight out of one of those films.) She came to the door and I was like 'what the f' is going on. Who is he and what the f' are you doing?'

Her reaction was (with an open mouth toothy smile on her face), 'Hey babe, what you doing here. Today is not your day.'

My reaction was my jaw dropping, and thinking would I get in trouble if I beat her down? 'Who's he', came out.

'My husband' (can I point out that she didn't look miffed at all, she acted like I was just the post boy delivering a package)

'Xxxx, what's going on? And who is he?'

'Oh sweetheart...' (That sounded degrading) *'That was my husband, and you need to leave. I will call you when I can.'*

'What do you mean- your husband? *What about us- what about me?'* What did she mean she was married and what the fuck was I still doing listening to this woman carry on?

With an irritated sign she carried on, *'Look leave, there is no us, you know that we were just fucking. No strings attached. Now leave.*

Oh God help me- It's wrong to want to beat her, right?

She carries on, 'Are you deaf? Leave- Look you knew I was married and was just looking for a hook up- that's all you where! Did you think there was anything more?'

'I'm in love you' (Yes I was pussy wiped, yes I was an idiot, and yes now looking back at it this is cringe worthy writing- WHAT THE HELL WAS WRONG WITH ME? SERIOUSLY! Any answers!!)

'Troy, I need you to leave. My husband is going out of town in two days- Lets meet up for a little one on one action then. But for now go. I will call you soon. Bye'

She shut the door and that was the last I saw her. She called me when her husband was out of town again. Turns out that as her husband travelled back and forth and mostly lived out of town Mrs. Bitchass Xxxxx would get bored, and initiate a new 'play-thing'. I was that play thing for that time. After that call I thought it would be wise for me to delete her number.

*

Matt thought it was funny and laughed me out. He told the rest of the guys, who still to this day take the piss out of me. Thank the Lord that they do it when Whitney or my sisters are not nearby. It's embarrassing enough without any of them knowing.

After Mrs. Bitchass Xxxx, I felt stupid and humiliated- who wouldn't! If I hadn't been on the receiving end of Mrs. Bitchass Xxxxx- *Emotionally Independent Fucker*, I wouldn't think of the negatives I would have nothing but all positives to say about these women.

As I believe that **they are smart, they take no prisoners and if you are stupid enough to get caught up and not**

take precaution with them, then that's on you. These women know what they want and they go for it. (Mrs. Bitchass Xxxxx- emotional fucker is a prime example)

***

These ladies do not allow themselves to get caught up in the moment and are ready to tell you so:

Ceela 29 dated her ex Antwone for close to a year. She broke up with him after he stopped talking to her for 2 days for apparently "dropping the phone on him." Ceela recounts the incident and says that Antwone acted like a kid as they had been in the midst of an argument when she told him she had no time to waste swapping words with him.

'I told him that I was getting off the phone and that he should call me when 'he was in a more reasonable mood'. I didn't see the problem with that. He knew how pissed I was and would have said something that I would later regret, so it was better that I got off the phone than stay on.

He didn't call me the next day, so I called him. He didn't pick up but sent me a text which read;

'Don't talk to me till you apologize for dropping the phone on me. That's straight up disrespectful.'

I told replied by telling him to 'grow the fuck up, grow a pair and that we were done!'

He called me thinking I was joking. I told him to 'lose my number from your phone and burn anything of mine I left at his place.'

He was" sorry" alright, he was quick with them but I had had enough.

He took the living piss!'

Brandy 33 wrote-

'I kicked my husband of 6 years out of the house after he told me I was being unreasonable. I told him to get a good divorce lawyer as I was taking everything from him including his pants. It was bad enough I was having a bad day, then he called me unreasonable- that was the last straw. I was searching for a reason to leave him and it didn't matter if my reason was reasonable or not. I was done with him ass. '

@NellyMelly24.net stated;

I told my boyfriend that he was too much of a mug for me. I could literally walk all over him. It became no fun anymore. I needed a new challenge.

- **When they are done, they are done.**

My baby buys me what I want when I ask him. And when he doesn't I kick up a fuss and I make him pay for rejecting my wants.'- **MsVandercamp1@********.co.uk**

The up side for their victims (the men) is that these women don't draw it out like men do. When they feel it's time to end the relationship, they end it regardless of how brutal it may be... And unlike men, these women give you the reason why you're being dumped.

@Kellyanonymous-lol wrote;

His head shape... Man he was sexy, great guy but I couldn't get over his head shape. It wouldn't have worked!! So I let him know. It was just a work fling anyways, but now anytime he sees me he jumps into the nearest room or broom closet just to avoid me. I am not embarrassed so why should he be- it was just a comment made to better himself and give his looks another 10% boost- if he fixed it (surgery works miracles)... Nothing is ever meant to last he should get that.

Don't get it twisted, if you're in a relationship with one of these women you will know. If you're just screwing then count your blessing as you could be in for a nightmare: *A money hungry nightmare.*

Like with any group truly brilliant, there is a dark side or better put an extreme side: And in context of the Emotionally Independent women you have the **"GOLDDIGGERS"**. As defined, golddigger (in context of what we are discussing) are women who place a higher interest and value on monetary and material benefits than the relationship at hand. *They care more for what they can* *get from the guy than a possible relationship developing between them.*

Golddiggers, as said, are the extreme and the most typically associated with the emotionally independent females out there. Even I modelled part of the definition of the emotionally independent female from the outlooks of golddigger's.

Golddiggers do not get emotionally involved or invested in any relationship; it's all about what they can get out of the relationship. These women have learned over time how to move past emotions within ANY relationship. (Basically they are emotionally stunted and learnt the trick of self preservation at an early stage of life)

They most likely learned to move past emotions after being hurt from one or two relationship(s): They felt like they put themselves way too out there just to get burnt. The first relationship in which they got hurt- their prides where knocked down but they built new barriers and put up more walls so that they "would never hurt the same again". The second relationship, he broke down her barriers slowly, he saw the hurt she was going through and understood as best as he could. But then that day came, she thought everything was good, or seemed good when he dumped her. This was the last thing she expected and could take:

Her faith in men- **damaged**

Her new motto- **'Fuck you before you fuck me!'**

She becomes jaded, and now is a man's worst but pleasantly best friend. For these women, caution should be taken as they can be really vicious, calculated and over achievers in the realm of manipulation sexual or not.

Cindy 33 went out with Marcus 40 for about 6 months:

Within those six months Marcus was paying my monthly rent, car payments and health insurance. 'I met Marcus at a club in Santana Row [California, San Jose]; he introduced himself to me as a broker, and stuck to me all night trying hard to get my number and buying me and my friends our drinks. He was cute, and his wallet was definitely my type. I gave him my number and the next day he called me and took me out for lunch.'

The first two months: *'By the end of the second week, he had announced to all that I was his girlfriend and he had taken me on two shopping trips and added my cell phone to his plan. By the end of the second month he was paying for my health insurance. I gave him a hand-job and a peck on the cheek to say thanks "as I wasn't that sort of girl".'*

Third and fourth month: *'Those months where a blur of gifts. More shopping, including a trip to New York for more shopping, he moved me into a nice apartment (closer to him) and was paying for the monthly rent. By this time I still hadn't slept with him. I told him I wasn't that type of girl and that I believed in no sex before marriage (that was a big lie but kept him from pushing me too hard).'*

Fifth and sixth month: *'He had proposed and told me he loved me by the end of the fifth month. The ring was nice but I wanted* bigger. We organised a party by the middle of the sixth month to celebrate our engagement.' (By this time I wanted out as he wanted more and I had a new boyfriend with a larger account than poor Marcus)

'I planned with Jenna [her best friend] for her to act flirty with Marcus all night while I got him drunk enough so that he would slip up and I would be there to catch him.'

It worked!

'I found them at a corner of the club with him trying to kiss her while groping her boobs. I acted outraged and dumped him that night.'

'He still pays for the car, my rent and health insurance and I kept the ring. He thinks that doing all of that will make me fall in love with him or allow us to get back together. Every now and again I do something to keep him locked onto me.'

Jenna 30, Cindy's best friend (and fellow extortionist) has been dating Danny 35 for the last year. She admits that she doesn't love him, but is with him "for his money". Jenna explains that Danny is a trust fund baby and buys her whatever she wants. 'After a few months of dating he moved me into his penthouse. He pays for everything. What more can a girl like me want!'

Lisa D 42 said,

'I have had boyfriends and been married. And what did I get from them, just bullshit and headaches. I say enough is enough.

> If I can get what I need and want from a guy without having to emotionally invest in him- then why not. "Milk em dry"'

SomeonepleasehelpBen.com

Ben a 32 year old budding actor (unwillingly admits to being a victim) went out with Linda 28 for two months. Within those two months Ben had bought Linda a £400 designer bag and the matching £250 designer shoes as she said that "she just had to have them". For her birthday, which was the second month they had been together Linda demanded that Ben throw her a "surprise" birthday party. When Ben declined Linda dumped him so Ben threw it.

The party set Ben [wannabe actor/ PA] back a few thousands and that wasn't including his gift. A week after the party Linda dumped Ben as she was 'seeing someone else'.

> Is it right for me to feel sorry for Ben or Marcus? Or think that brought it on themselves?

- ### In The confines of a relationship

    So, how do these women- the emotionally stunted few, deal with being in a relationship? Do they bulk like their Alpha male counter parts when things get too serious? Do they even embrace the thought of being tied down to another for any lengths of time?

LT 35 (my cousin) till recently had not had a long lasting relationship. I think her longest relationship is this recent one of 2 years and a few months, which recently ended when her ex had cheated on her. LT finds it hard being in a relationship as she doesn't believe she is one of those women to be locked down too long in any relationship. 'I love my freedom and the fact that I don't have to "report" back to any man.... The only reason I went out with the fool, was because I thought it was about time that I could say I understood what it was like to be in a relationship. Now I know, and I don't think am missing anything from not being in one.

Good riddance to bad rubbish.'

In relationships women of this group are less likely to believe that they are equals to their partners.

LT- 'When I was with that cheating bastard he was a crutch on her nerves. I wanted and still want more from life and he was "just ok" with his circumstances. He was a mid level assistant manager of a phone store- what's to be 'ok' with that!

He should have been reaching to be better and do better than that: He has been that mediocre assistant manager for the best part of two years.... When we first got together, he had just become an assistant manager and was finishing off at school. I was a supervisor, still at school. I graduated and found a part-time career job and stayed at the supervisor job but as a part-timer, he carried on as an assistant manager. I moved onto a full time position in my career job and he finally graduated.... I think that was what really got me about him, he was just ok with being a mid level assistant store manager; he used to want more. I liked that about him, we were always talking about what we wanted and how we would go about getting it. He settled and it became embarrassing as I earned twice more than he ever did.'

There is always a power play within the dynamic of the relationship for which the partners of these women are always playing the defensive side, as opposed to the attack: Without a doubt they are antagonistic.

LT- 'The cheating arsehole would - now and again- try and put his foot down or try and act in a way that I thought was controlling. He would try to give me orders. Once he told me that I wasn't allowed to go to a friend's birthday party, (this friend happened to be an on again off again 'fuck feast' who I had told him about when we had started dating- we where currently off at this point) I laughed in his face and told him 'he was funny'. I went to the party. The next day he was sulking.... It's like this- I don't like to feel controlled, I give you your respect but then you think you can throw your weight about when it concerns me? He was really a dumb motherfucker to think he could do battle with me...

...His ex called him once, to invite him to a party that she was hosting. I told him 'if you think you're going- think otherwise. Double standards I know- but his ex wanted him back bad and would have done anything to get her hands on him.'

'... He tried to argue, but I shut that down- as always.'

- **Their partners**

    The partners (boyfriends, girlfriends-whatever's) these females tend to attract are of equal educational and working backgrounds. Therefore the more successful she is, the more successful her partner would be. These women are affluent or working their way up to be at a reasonable level of prosperity; they are the career focused women that put the job first and family second. (They tend to start their families later than any of the other women.)

LT states;

'While with that fool, I became an Accounts Exec for a large international company based in the States, he on the other hand, is still an assistant store manager getting pittance for pay. If not for him cheating I think I would have dumped him for the fact that he was in a dead end job going nowhere in life. Plus it would be embarrassing to tell anyone what he did for a living.'

Jamelia 39 wrote;

'I think what sealed the deal and why I married my husband was that, even though I was his boss he still aspired to reach my level and surpass it. I tell him there's no competition between us- though, if there were I would be winning it hands down.'

Melissa 45-I am a doctor and my husband is a surgeon... I stay in control of my house and wear the pants (so to say between us).'

Aarella 38 stated;

My partner Angela is a professor of humanities and I am an associate professor in Criminal Justice. I hopefully will be on the tenure track next year. But thinking of it, I don't think that I could be with another woman who wasn't of the same or above experience as me. That's what attracted me first to Angela- I find a woman in an authority position sexy and it helps that she is a knock out herself.

Nells 33 wrote in, 'I got rid of my boyfriend after he got fired from his job. I found him literally unattractive the day he stopped wearing his power suits and started wearing sweat pants everywhere. Sloppy'

- **Not in a Relationship**

@Tejannet29 stated;

'... We are the realist's- Nothing lasts forever... Men come and go so you might as well make use of them while they are about!'

When I first started off collecting data and researching for this read my first thought was that as the term emotional Independents rightly suggests these women who are emotionally independent prefer their independence than to waste time attempting to form attachments let alone emotional attachments of any lengths.

I now disagree, I think that these women a more likely to be picky than the rest. They don't just settle with anyone. He has to be right in every sense of the way.

Anna 39

'I once dated this guy; he had this nervous tick about him that I actually liked as he loved to play with my breasts. He was a boob man and I liked that even more about him....Then

I caught him playing with his nipples while he was doggy-style fucking me. It was weird and I freaked out. I mean I turned around and he had his eyes closed, his hands playing with his nipples while fucking me. I freaked and told him that I had to leave as it was my aunt's birthday and my family had plans that I couldn't miss.'

'Yeah I didn't call him back...EVER....

I mean, I like freaky men and I am open to new things and experiments BUT that was gross.'

He had moobs- man boobs ewww. No. I said Bye as soon as I saw him. - @iaintpickie.net

Denise24*****@******.com *wrote;*

My ex became my ex as I got tired of him and his excuses. I told him to 'go see a doctor' as he could only get it up once before he got too tired or before he complained about something or the other. I have needs and he wasn't satisfying me. At all!

Charlie said

'...I have noticed that my girlfriend Emma dumps me anytime it's her turn to spend money on me. She picks a fight just to dump me or just dumps me; a week later she calls me saying she misses me. We get back together and the cycle continues. It's Valentine's Day in a month's time; I wonder what she's going to do.'

Charlie, Charlie, Charlie. Let's move on....

Evelyn said

'I once dated a guy who was too much of a mummy's boy. I felt like I was dating him and his mother. He would tell his mother everything; we had sex and he would tell her, we had an argument- he would tell her and well she would call me. After two months of it, I broke up with him and his mother.'

In a random conversation with Ellen 32 on the train (who happened to be reading over my shoulder on the notes I had been making on this chapter and this section)....

'I admit that I am picky when it comes to the men I allow in my lives. But would you really date someone who looked like they hadn't bathed or combed their hair in a year?'

Ellen's mum had set her up on a blind date with some Dr Dude from her church:

'I only went out with him to shut her up about how single I was and so that she could stop telling her friends, family members and our Minister that 'I preferred my toys than the feel of a real man'.

How embarrassing- I mean, my mum does this all the time. She likes to make me squirm with embarrassment. Once, when I had just turned 15, my mum tried to pay my hot neighbour to teach me how to kiss. The next day he told everyone at school. I was humiliated.'

> At this point I let out a snort of laughter, Ellen looks at me pissed... 'I'm sorry- where's my manners, please carry on' I said feeling embarrassed.

Ellen- *'Anyways, this Dr Dude may have earned great money and seemed nice to talk to on the phone but he looked like shit in person.*

I felt too embarrassed to sit in public and be seen with him. So I did the fake-a-call emergency thing and left....He called me the next day and I told him I wasn't interested in him: 'It's you not me and it just won't work'. That night mum called me. I told her what happened and she said I was vain- imagine.'

Me Vain!

'She [Ellen's mother] said, I was too fussy, and needed to move past my vibrators. She said that if I didn't get my ass out of my "list" I would never find a good guy or even a decent one who would want me for me.'

<In a voice which I think was mimicking her mother she say's>

'...he may be standing right in front of you like Dr Dude guy. Or, he may be giving you a good lick-down and you wouldn't know as you're too stuck up and can act like such a bitch.'

'I was mortified my mum said "lick-down".'

Kelly 50 admits that the 'smallest flaw in a man is enough to end a seemingly perfect relationship with him.' She says that that's an issue she has been dealing with for years but it can't be helped. 'Even my therapist thinks am a lost cause.'

Lilly 27 said'

'I feel like am settling, I wasn't made to just settle with anyone. If I could find or if the perfect man did really exit then maybe I would settle. But for now I will nitpick through any possible guy till I find someone who fits into my idea of perfection personified.'

Lana 29

'I found the perfect man that gets me, he understands me well. I can find no fault with him- as his my vibrator.'

- **The single life is better?**

    These women are what you may typically call commitment phoebes: This is true to an extent due to their nitpicking antics. They find faults when things start to look serious within a relationship some find faults and move on.

Remember Anna 39...

No I didn't dump nipple gate guy because I was getting serious with him. I broke up with him because of that incident. We didn't date for that long, only for a couple of months in which we only had full on sex that once. Once was enough for me.

Lana 29...

'The last guy I went out with was over a year ago. I broke up with him as things where moving 'faster than I was ready for. He was talking marriage and babies and I wasn't up for that.

Kelly 50

I was engaged once, but that ended two weeks before I walked down the aisle. All I kept thinking was that I couldn't see myself locked down with this guy till one of us died or got fed up with each other. At least I didn't leave it till the day of the wedding- am not one of those runaway brides you hear of.

- **He is set to fail**

    Most likely single as they set high standards for potential partner(s): Cynical group as there is no belief of 'the one', but a belief of finding someone tolerable enough with all the ticks on the list against their name. He may not be perfect but at least he does what he needs to do.

Ellen 32 chooses to be single and endure her mother's futile attempts of setting her up, as she would rather sort out her life and work track than deal with the hassle of relationships and the commitments and flexibility involved. Ellen prefers the fuck buddy system, 'that way I can keep my fussy nitpicking antics to a low. He just has to be good in the sack.'

- **Dumpers Dumpees**

    In your case ladies you can either be the ones doing the dumping, which is more likely or you also can be the ones being dumped (less likely). Many reasons come to play if we are referring to the latter of the last statement, as we will find out from Georgina and Lauren.

    Being dumped for these ladies is *'no biggie as shit happens and some relationships are not meant to be.'* – *Camilla 33*

They are the best break artist and are more likely to get over the supposed heart ache faster than any other the other ladies as remember- they are the realists and more pragmatic of the groups.

Georgina 38-

'My motto is, 'if I don't get caught then whatever I'm doing can't be considered as cheating'. Unfortunately for him, my soon to be ex husband (papers still being filed) thought otherwise when he walked in on me and my brother in law (his sister's husband) having sex. He went into a rage; I tried to explain to him that I didn't see anything wrong with my behaviour but that didn't seem to work. Oh well!'

Lauren 42 states;

'I have been married for 21 years, and I finally told my husband how I really felt about his jokes- they weren't funny and could be considered offensive... Well, I think that was his last straw with me as we have been separated for the last 4 ½ months. I actually prefer the separation: Am thinking it should become more permanent. It's not like we weren't having problems, but I think he finally had enough of me and my bluntness, or more likely me.'

- **Hyper sexuality or just active sex lives**

    This category of females are either very sexually active with regular fuck buddies. They are the most sexually aggressive and most likely to be very sexually adventurous. They are the *Samantha's* of the female population.

Stella 27-

'...If I call you in the middle of the night, it's for one thing and one thing only. So please lets skip the small talk when I get to your place. Don't tell me how your day has been as I DON'T CARE. And yeah as soon as we are done and am satisfied, am leaving to go home; and I will call you when next I may need some servicing.'

Bernie 28 'I live and breathe by the fuck buddy system. Relationships suck!'

Gill, 30

It's like that saying- 'once you go black...', but once you start 'no strings attached' you want nothing more. It works for me- don't think I will be starting any new long-term relationships anytime soon.

Terry 25

'....Those films got it wrong; you don't hook up with the fuck buddy in the end... You just keep fucking him.'

- **The type of partner that they go for**

    As previously stated their partners are of equal educational and working backgrounds, but then, this group of women has no distinct type of men they go for unlike the other groups: For them, opposites do attract, and the similar he is to you then the better. The guy can be a push over or arrogant just as long as he knows what his doing with himself and not along for a bullshit field ride.

5. And the Mixtures are In, Introducing the...

Due to the fact that I have already introduced you all to the more prominent subsidiaries of the Emotionally Co-Dependent females, I feel there is no point me further regurgitating what's been said and move on to introducing you to some of the characters from the Emotionally Co-Dependent subsidiaries.

I should mention that the reason why we look at the mixtures in the order of Co-Dependent with additives of either Dependent and Independent traits is due to the fact that the co-dependent category holds the two more prominent and common subsidiaries.

- **The exhaustive Emotionally Co- Dependent with Hints of Emotionally Dependent extracts**

<u>The Emotionally Co-Dependent Dependent females</u>- "I know the answer, I know how to solve my problem BUT it's easier said than done.... If you were in my shoes you would better understand but as you're not, you can't understand.... It's just too hard to let go of what we share, **though I know I should... I know he is no good for me** *but I'm just here till I can find a way out of this relationship."*

Their motto's: *'Talk is cheap and actions speak louder than words.'*

Out of any other group, these women **do not live up to their motto.** They are truly misunderstood due to this. *Their motto's hold no worth in these women's lives though they imply and impose these views on others.* The words are simply aesthetics; they are face value words that are easily said for show. It's all just talking it up for these ladies.

- The talkers- "talk is cheap"

The Emotionally Co-Dependent Dependent women are infuriating. **They are the women who know what they should do, but decide otherwise and then whine about the outcomes.**

It's all about the **knowing** for these women. *They know what they have to do but shy away from it.* They can talk about and around what they are going to do **but they do not take or make that move.**

All talk and no action!

These women do not have the "gift of the gab" but can talk you around their relationship problems. They tell you what the problems is, what they want to do and are going to do about that problem but renege on their decision as they are simply too scared to make such a stance.

Danielle, T states:

... It's bad I know, but I can't count how many times that I've told my friends that I would leave him (him being my boyfriend Mike) but it's hard. I don't love Mike as I used to but I feel bad to just break up a 3 year relationship. I think he may soon propose to me as he has been leaving hints about the house and hinting to friends, plus he has been talking to my dad more of late...

Alice, B writes:

What's the male equivalent to a mistress? Man- stress?

Well I have one of those: I have been married two years now and have had my "man fling/ man-stress" for that same length of times as well. I have talked it over with myself (as I can't tell anyone else- my friends are real blabber mouths, plus it's hard to explain my situation) and I need to get rid of one of them!

But, which one do I choose?

I don't know! I love them both.

@Trinity36&confused stated:

'I have a friend like this, who is the biggest talker alright! She has been telling us for about a year now how 'she is about to dump her shitty boyfriend'. She has said this countless times, and moans constantly about how her boyfriend doesn't do this and does that; how dirty he is and how much she's tired of his nonsense.

The last time she complained was a week ago. No change has occurred.

They are still together, no matter what she says she will stay with him till one of them keels over. She is just a broken record of **shoulda coulda woulda's.**

June 32, her story:

'I used to live in Miami with my boyfriend; well he was actually my fiancé till we broke up due to his commitment issues. (He didn't want to get married, he just wanted me as his arm piece- his go to girl) When I finally broke it off with him, I moved back home to Jersey.

That only lasted two months. Trevor called me saying he was 'sorry and missed me and was ready to set a date and get the wedding ball rolling'.

By the way that was his then "proposal"!

That was four years ago, and I'm still his girlfriend and now his unofficial fiancé.

I admit that I'm stuck. What am I to do? I could leave him, **but it's hard as I love him.**

I know he doesn't want what I want. His already told me that he doesn't want to get married, his actual words being: **'Why buy the cow when you can get the milk for free.'** Imagine how those words made me feel!

I want more, I want kids and to get married- the full works.

I want out, and have been saying it for a while though I'm still here.

- ### The Katie's of the world- *Confussed.com*

Katie is a 26 year old paralegal who had been, for the last two years in a relationship with Adam. In her many years of dating, Katie's had only two serious relationships and the others she classifies as "nothing but failed mistakes and sexual deviations."

Before Adam and I were together, I was more independent and self reliant. But that changed slowly... I began to feel and think that I needed Adam... and couldn't be without him.

It all became about him. I lost myself in a relationship that I wanted out of.

I wasn't being true to myself being with him, if I remember correctly *I would ask myself at times: Do I really want him? Do I really love him? What are you really with him?*

My answers were always skewed and never a definite yes, there was no logical answer why I was with him. I remember thinking one time what I was going to do if he wasn't about.

My decisions were always based on the thinking of 'I need a man' and 'I want this relationship more than him.'

I was just hurting myself as *I felt that I had failed myself*, and so was therefore obligated to be in a relationship, this relationship. He was my second chance at getting it right, and making a lasting relationship.

I confess *I was in love with the idea of being in love, of being in a relationship: A fully functioning relationship. I didn't even like him from the get go.*

He was the only guy that I had tried to work through all the short comings and problems. We had issues... **He had issues and I stayed and really tried to make things work. I should have left a long time ago- instincts told me better but my brain and heart stopped communicating.**

- **"Numbers ... Numbers .... Numbers"**

    As a man in this day and age, it is easy for me to say that I have slept with 15 different women: Out of the 15- 5 of them I was in relationships with for at least a year or two and the others consisted of one night stands, fuck buddies and the general 'near to relationship status- *'let's see where this is going' flings'.*

    BUT for some women this is different. The amount of numbers **signifies** differently to them the older they become, especially if they are still single.

    For these ladies, it's all in the numbers, putting weight on these numbers and implying a negative connotation to the fact that they have slept with this amount of men and are still looking for "Mr Right".

    Therefore, as the numbers increase in men they have slept with the more emphasis on creating a longer lasting relationship that has no real basis on love, affection and even like.

Jennifer A

In retrospect my last two and only relationships, only became full blown relationships after I gave up the goods too soon or sooner than I wanted to.

I don't think I sleep around but I am embarrassed to admit that in my 27 years I have slept with 10 guys, 2 of which were semi serious relationships.

I have been asked several times how many guys I've slept with and as soon as I say the number I can feel the recipient of the conversation judging me and thinking that am a **slut**.

I recently became single again and I have vowed that **guy number 11 is going to be my husband and father of my children.** My friend laughs and says that <u>I am too obsessed and fixated on the numbers and not the quality of the relationships, and that's why I have found myself in dead end relationships.</u>

@MaraLa Bon.net writes;

'I am only admitting this as no one will [know] it's me... but **I have slept with 9½ guys in the 10 years that I have been sexually active.** <u>I look back now and wish I had slowed my role... Only in recent years have I understood what sleeping with this number of guys implies.</u>

Oh- the half was my first girl on girl experience, so I don't think it counts as there was no penetration... just all fingers, tongue and a dildoe with a plug.

Tina 34

I'm 34 and thank goodness married. I have three kids and another on the way and feel no way in telling them (if ever asked) that in my life I have only slept with one man- my husband. I do have friends that are still single and are married who can't use both fingers and toes to count their sexual partners; I have no problems in that as long as they are doing it safely.

Brian 26

I am the 19th guy my girlfriend has slept with. I had a real problem when she told me this as I thought it made her seem loose: Till she told me that she had [incurred] those numbers after being in several group orgies and threesomes with pervious partners.

I think that ROCKS personally and I am trying to get her to do one with me (and hopefully her sex best friend).

Anil 46

Before I married my wife I had been with 7 different women (all but 2 I had been in relationships with), but when I found out that she had been with more (mostly out of relationships) I had a problem with that. I actually felt sickened with her number (14) and called her a whore.

I later apologized many times over that. But I am still disturbed by the number.

Jillonetoomany23@*****.net

I love sex but I admit that I also too have been in relationships so that I can have regular sex. For me I have some liking to my boyfriends not love but it beats having a high count in partners.

I don't want to meet the perfect guy and have to tell him that I have had more than 5 sexual partners: Am currently on 3 and definitely not going past 5.

"Danita U 33 & Sexy" stated;

'How many have you had Troy?

... Well I have had 30 and counting. No I am not a porn star or whore; I am just a woman with needs that incur regular tapping and sexual partners. Yes I stated partners- Plural. My therapist thinks my sexual exploits is due to the fact that I have 'daddy issues'. **BULL!**

I just think it's good to have a variety as you should always have choices.'

*

@Danita, I think that your therapist hit the mark!

As previously stated, I put nothing to the numbers as in this day and age relationships are not made to last as they once did. Sexual liberation for women has enabled the boundaries of monogamous relationships to be blurred from the traditional classic views. So having sex with multiple partners while in or out of a relationship is seen as a norm in today's society.

**

While writing this section I decided to ask both Whitney and Leyton how many guys they had been with for **_"insightful" purposes_**. And to see if I could finally get the truth from Whitney who never seemed to tell me her actual count.

I didn't delve into the topic straight; I started by massaging her neck- *'Oh! So stressed, Babe you want me to run you a bubble bath?*

'Yeah sure,' she kisses me. 'How was your day?' She asks.

'Good, Good. Um just was discussing some of my research with Regina. We were discussing some of my findings.'(Which was a total lie as after Regina's big mouth told everyone in the office about Mrs. Xxxx you really think I would let her in on this.)

'Oh what findings are these', she asks.

Dig deep and go in for the kill- *'About sex and how many sexual partners women normally have.... So- Babe, just curious... What's your count?'*

I look at her, smile and kiss the top of her head. She looks up into my eyes; smiles back then twists her lips as she always does when thinking. She squints her eyes and I know am fucked.

What Whitney implied from my simple question- *'So... What, you think as I gave it up on our first real date that that means I've slept with all other dates I've had? Do you want the number to include female partners?'*

That's a trick question- So **DO NOT REPLY. Whatever you do don't nod.**

I nodded, Shit. How did that happen? I told my brain not to move.

She moves away from my hold, looks at me, *'If you were ready for the number I would have told you by now'*, then walked out the room.

Again, no answer just another diversion tactic from Whit which made me feel crappy by the end. *No sex that night!*

When I asked Leyton, she was open with that. *'Matt would be the 3rd guy I have slept with,'* was her simply response.

***

- ### And then you have the RUNNERS

If we where to look in any high school year book under the labels of most likely to **run or shy away from a problem or situation and least likely to succeed within a low to medium stressor situation,** you would find these women there.

These women do not cope well within any semblance of a stressful relationship. ***They won't quit the relationship as that is out of the question due to their ideology of love and what it means to have a failed relationship.***

Arguments when they occur are handled by these women in a juvenile and fairly improper fashion- they do not know how to properly deal with the argument or the reality of what the argument may signify so they run, pretend and ignore the situation and problems at hand.

They front- put up pretence, (they are the Teresa's of the world) which at best is weak.

My loves' we all can see through this act.

This group of women have no sense of reasonability; they feel that talking out and attempting to sort out the smallest of problems has no effect, so instead of dealing they **cower away** and (you guessed it) **RUN**.

Outtake of a conversation between sisters- Tina and Lauren from London (no ages or initial given);

Tina- 'My sister tells me that I run away from dealing with my problems than face it as I can't handle the truth or deal with it. I don't think it's that, I just think that as much as I talk about the issue at hand and all the talking gets nowhere, there is no need to deal or face it again as it only brings up more problems. Jay (my boyfriend) and I argue like normal couples but sometimes I just need space... regardless of our problems.'

Lauren- 'No, what you do Tina is, instead of dealing with the issue which are always minor you run and hide which in turn escalates the problem from minor to major. You need to learn to deal with your problems head on than running away as it doesn't help. All it does is burying it momentarily and increase your anxiety.'

The only difference between these women and the Emotionally Dependent women is that the Emotionally Co Dependent Dependents **know** that their relationships have persistent problems. But then, the clear similarity between both groups is that instead of dealing with the problems they cower and give up resulting in the Emotionally Co-Dependent Dependents running and the Emotionally Dependents "sticking through" and staying like die harder's.

- ## His only with you for the money

    Let's see; do you remember in the previous chapter of the Emotional Dependent females when we looked at *"the ones likely to get used"*?

    Ok well like the Emotional Dependents, the Emotionally Co Dependent Dependents unfortunately are not immune to this treachery from their partner(s).

    <Side note: I am not disputing that other women of the other groups do not see this happen to them, as in fact women from all categories are susceptible to fraudulent partners but what I am saying is that the above groups mentioned (The Emotionally Dependent and The Emotionally Co- Dependent Dependents) are the groups of women more likely to have this happen to them.>

    June 41 stated;

'Looking back it's easier to laugh at such a situation as I knew he was using me for my money as I flaunted it in his face. I didn't care at the time and to an extent don't now though I wish I would have been a lot wiser with my choices in men:

I was 24, young dumb and totally in love with a dipshit who I bought a car for. No- truth be told- My parents gave me the money for the car as my birthday [present] and I gave it to my boyfriend at the time as I wanted him to like and love me more. He liked me more alright, as I would give him gifts and money as he wanted and asked for them.

He dumped me when my parents cut me off once they found out what I was doing.

Janice W said;

'My [ex] asked me to help him once to get his car out of the impound lot. When I went to pick it up I had to pay close to £2000 because of charges and the surcharges he accumulated by leaving his car there for so long. He said he would pay me back when he was good. I'm guessing he never got good as he always wanted me to do him a favour and it always included money. It's not like I didn't know what I was doing; it's just that I let it happen.'

Serena M said;

'It started off as a good will gesture as my boyfriend was out of work, now am paying nearly all his bills and my bills. I get paid more than him so he believes that it's cool for me to handle most of 'our bills' as he puts it.

I thought it was a good gesture and would be temporary but I tried to get out of it when he started work we ended up having a big row which resulted in him saying 'if I loved him enough I would not make a big deal out of paying the bills.'

I don't know how to get out of it without breaking our relationship.'

- **The one's with borderline ABANDOMENT ISSUES**

    We have all met one of these types. Let me self correct: We have all somehow somewhere interacted with these "abandonment issue filled women"- *the ones always praying and begging that he won't leave them.*

    At all cost their fear is *'that the only guy that really may love me might leave me if I do not do as he says or wants.'*

@April****** stated

'I wasn't over reacting with these feeling that he would leave me. It was and still is a natural feeling that when you get into a relationship with a guy that you really like that you would up and just leave you. And he did- I was right to feel that way.'

'I meet "Mr. Maybe right" and it turns out that he finds me to "Mrs. No Way in Hells Chance". Damn right I feel like he will leave me. They normally do. I think I come on way too strong at first. After the first date I tend to cyber stalk and tell them how I *feel and the fact that I want kids- and how our kids would look like.'- Mary C, 24 from Vancouver*

Csilover4ever wrote;

'I get scared that he will leave. I can't imagine my life without him..... I love him more than I have loved anyone else in my life. I don't ever want to be without him.'

- **The ones who change their appearances**

    I remember when Leyton first got with Matt; she was a peacock. One of the rarities, a black girl who **understood** that she did not need to wear extensions, weaves, or even have a chemical perm to straighten her natural locks. She was a natural brunette, well that was till Matt interrupted her life and made her change all that within the first month they became a couple. No more brunette but a black dye job on a head of chemically permed and straightened hair, with weave extensions to make her hair fuller. *The first time I saw her after all that and the makeup, I didn't recognize her. I mean she looked great, but it wasn't Leyton.*

    I wouldn't have changed a thing about her. I like my girls natural and themselves- no additives.

    I asked her what the big change was all due to; *she told me that Matt had said that '[she] would look better and he would find her more attractive with permed hair with a "darker finish" and an introduction to some makeup.'*

'He doesn't like it when my hair is in braids, or when I wear my hair naturally so I started perming It.' she said, and further stated that;

'He thinks that when I wear red it makes me look fat, so I stopped wearing red though it's my favourite colour. I can't even wear red lipstick or lip gloss.'

Changing your appearance for your partners benefit and to your disadvantage is questionable for me.

AnneLaurie***@****.com stated;

When I got with my boyfriend, he hated my hair long and kept telling me that I should cut it. I hadn't had my hair short since I was young, and I wore my hair long to hide my ears as they stick out like elf ears... For his birthday he demanded that I get my hair cut short, he even had a clipping of a short pixie cut that he liked. He said my hair cut would be his perfect present. That was a year back, since then he doesn't allow me grow my hair more than a few inches from the cut. I have to get trims regularly to keep him happy.

In a conversation with **Li 25, who has been with her fiancé for 6 years:**

Spray tan! I never ever used spray tan till I met my fiancé. He thinks am too pale, so he gets me to spray tan regularly. One month I spray tanned so much that I looked like an orange blob; it came off on my sheets and clothes. It was nasty.

Laura N 36 from North London wrote on my blog;

I started waxing my bikini line some years back. But then when I got with my current boyfriend he didn't like hair down there and wouldn't perform orals until I got it clear... I find it weird and I have to keep on top of the waxing as when it starts to grow back... it itches likes the shits down there.

Sharon T 43 said;

I wear fake nails and eye lash extensions... My husband likes them, he has always liked them: He was the one that got me into it. He says they make my fingers look longer and sexier. And my eyelashes bring out my natural eye colour the longer they are- I personally don't see the difference except I wear a lot of mascara now than before. I have to wear them now all the time as my own nails are too brittle and my eyelashes are messed or nonexistent to be out on display.

- **Emotionally Co-DEPENDENT with a swish of Independence and crazy!!!**

<u>AforAnonymous#1 wrote</u>; 'How about this, the craziest thing I did was walk into the empty disabled toilets at work- lock it down where I masturbated after a 2 hour meeting I had where I was swapping dirty messages between one of my sexy co workers and also my boyfriend (all at the same time and never got caught out). I was so heated after the exchanges that I soaked my panties and went into the bathroom to finish off. After I finished I took an early lunch and went in search of my boyfriend to finish off the work that he and my co worker had started.

> **<u>The Emotional Co-Dependent Independents females</u>**- These women are independent of their relationship(s), but still love and enjoy the security it provides. **They embrace their freedom but at the same time would rather <u>choose</u> being in a relationship or some sort of companionship just to see what they could get out of it.** These women are close relatives of the golddigger's.

Their motto: 'Been there done that, but why not give it another try, this time my way!'

Okay, Ladies and Gents think what you want on the Emotionally Independent females but, for me I think that the Emotionally Co-Dependent Independent group of females are crazier, a little more disturbed and on edge than any other group or subsidiary.

At least with the Independent crowd you knew and understood to an extent what you where getting or dealing with. With this group of women ... **ALWAYS**

EXPECT THE UNEXPECTED- which at times is not a good thing, though sexually speaking- as you will find out they are real Kinks.

A term that should be associated to this subsidiary group is *emotional terrorists.* The reason to this association is that these women unlike the emotionally independents have more tolerance- They can see the signs of a sinking relationship and instead of cutting their losses straight off (emotional independents) they stay in it out of **choice**.

They **can** see that their boyfriend/ partner/ other half is readying to quite. **But will** find a way to reel him back in **till she is ready** to dispose of him as she wants. For these ladies, reeling or keeping him in check till she is ready to split is an easy task. It's all about manipulations and tricks- allow him into believing what you want him to.

Ed stated 45: 'my ex and I where together for 4 years. We never got married or had kids but the manipulative bitch took my house, the things in it and kicked me out. I was stupid enough to add her name on the deed and ownership papers but not mortgage and bill payments'- So I still pay and she lives there cosy with her new boyfriend.

*ToniMW26@*****.COM wrote,*

'Keon had this crazy idea that he could get one by me. Little did he know! He started seeing someone from work and thought I didn't know. I played along with his games for an extra three months: I allowed him to treat me to the extra gifts his guilt was

buying me. He didn't see it coming when I emptied our joint bank account and moved back home to Canada.'

- ### I hear what you say but I'm not listening

    Say what you have to say to these ladies and then be done. As, as much talking and nagging and bitching you do these women will still do as they want.

    *

    Ladies of all groups, question;

    Have you got one of those friends that you can turn to when in need of advice and some guidance as they always help you put things into perspective plus they have the look of having their shit together?

    If your answer is – YEAH, then I have another question:

    Ever tried to return the favour of giving them some guidance when you see they are having a hard time and in need of it, and had it shut down in your face?

    Your answer is most likely yes. You know why?

    As great advice and guidance givers these women are, they are bad at receiving advice from others or even taking their own advice.

Luanne 46, 'Am not one to openly go out there and give advice. My friends do come to me for my thoughts and inputs and am okay with that, but when I was getting my divorce I had people telling me everything was going to be ok and that I would get through it. How are they to know this when I didn't see the divorce coming. I was blindsided by my husband who took everything from me. **They didn't know how I felt or how it felt to be in that situation. So when they were trying to advice me and such... I told them all where to go.'**

Lucy 25, 'Nana, great girl and friend... But I feel that it's easy for her to dish it out. She always knows what to say and the right advice to give. But when she was on the receiving end, couldn't take it. She was in constant denial and refused to listen or take the same advice she would give me when she was in similar situations to mine. Nana's still with her fiancé even though his trying to pressure her into moving to Kenya so that they can start their family there and get married. I get that he works for some company located there, but I keep telling her that he's only thinking of himself and she needs to think about what she wants; Which is to stay here [California] and not to relocate to a place where she has no family or friends or even a job.'

Tina 33, 'I give advice as- I am asked. So, when I don't ask please **DO NOT FEEL FREE TO GIVE IT, as I will shut you down.'**

Fiona 29 'My boyfriend says he hates it when I braid my hair. I told him that his feelings of what I do to my hair are totally irrelevant to our relationship and if he hated my braids he could hop skip and Willie Bounce outta me face.'

- **Feel my raft**

Ok, so we established that the women of the Emotional Co-Dependent Independent group are a force upon themselves. So you can imagine what pissing them off would be like.

<u>Scary!</u>

They take no prisoner, that's a fact.

Marcus White 37 wrote on my blog-

'My wife once shredded my one of a kind signed Lakers jersey after me and the guys were meant to go away for a week but ended up staying for an extra two weeks. She was so pissed. I turned off my phone after she kept ringing it off. I wanted to have fun and catch up with the boys.

As much as the extra time with the guys was worth it- my jersey was one of a kind **and she just told me that I deserved what she did and she would do more if I kept complaining.'**

Jenny W 30

I paid my cousin to key the outside of my ex's car, break into it and slash the interior. It felt good planning it. I knew how much he loved the car so when he called me crying... I told him to 'piss off and go back to one of his bum bitches that he cheated on me with'...Before I dropped the call, I told him that I wasn't surprised that this happened and he got what was coming to him. Till this day he doesn't know I was the one that orchestrated it.

I haven't heard from the police either.'

Chris 45 states;

'My wife once caught me masturbating to a picture of her sister. She threatened to cut off my man if she ever caught me doing it again. The embarrassing thing is that she told her sister, who thought it would be great to tell everyone and anyone about it so that they could all laugh at me.'

Pamela 55

'I found out that my husband was sleeping with my sister so I broke her noise and cracked a few of his ribs and broke his ring finger as a symbol. It was worth the assault charge. Divorced him and forgot her.'

@Vanessa.net wrote;

'I once told an ex that I would lace his food with rat poison and arsenic. We were arguing and he was really starting to grate on my nerves. So I told him that. He freaked out, and dumped me. At least then we stopped arguing.

He called me a crazy bitch- I took it as a complement.'

- **Queue the DRAMA**

    These women may have in another life been drama major's or are so now, for a simple argument for these women is never as it seems. The argument may be over something so insignificant as "which side of the bed you sleep on" to a more pressing subject as your sex life and personal ethics but you ladies will make it seemed bigger than it is. **You embellish, expand and exaggerate the truth for outcomes we men still do not *understand*.**

Jared Lee M, 43

I decided it was in my best interest to file for divorce from my crazy bitch of an ex wife. ***The reason I stated when filling for divorce was irreconcilable differences as they didn't have a section for crazy ass drama orientated women like her.*** *I think our relationship maybe construed as abuse from her as she thought it was wise to constantly throw tantrums and smash whatever was in sight on the floor, twice the flower pot and lamp on my head and a knife to my memory foam pillow **as I forgot to do the food shopping.** But how was I supposed to remember after I had a day full of meetings and she was at home doing nothing.*

Elise B states

*'I don't know how to answer this question and section as **I admit I have argued unnecessarily, exaggerated and embellished all or most arguments, disagreements with my other half. I have no problem admitting it as it helps me get my way and it gets me out of trouble.***

<u>My penance for drama got me out of getting caught cheating once:</u>

Barry came home early from work unexpectedly a month ago and found me in a compromising situation with our Church Pastor- We had been kissing and his hand had wondered into my cleavage when Barry walked through the door. By the time he found us my bra was on display and my lipstick was all but smeared.

When he saw both our appearances I burst into tears, ran to him and told him that I had just had a vision and had called the pastor over as my vision put us in danger. He asked why my bra and lipstick where as they where and I told him that I had another vision while the pastor was there and the vision had gotten crazy. He didn't ask anymore but that was a close call... *since then the Pastor and I have been careful- Hotels are so cliché but easy for dalliances.'*

Kelly 28 states

'I don't think I over react when we argue, though Tyrone thinks I do. **He calls me a drama queen as he says that am very argumentative, stubborn and explosive at the most inappropriate things and times. The last argument we had was this morning when he wouldn't kiss me due to "my morning breath".**

I woke up turned around to him thinking it would be romantic to wake him up with a kiss. It was like he sensed my lips coming towards him and turned around, so that my face was to his back. I thought that was f****d up. So **I hit him awake and all hell ensued from my mouth**.'

Christine 45 wrote on my blog

'May be I am inclined to the dramatics: It can't be helped. My ex broke up with me as he said that at times I treated our relationship and my life as if it's a soap opera. He said that I brought way too much drama into his life that he was ready to switch it up and get me out of his life.'

Chi Chi wrote in;

Darren thinks that I'm drama. He claims that I thrive in it to make his life 'something close to a living nightmare'. He says that constantly and we argue about that and also why his still with me.

I once got really mad at him while we were having (yes during) sex as he switched up positions just before I came. If he had carried on in that position I would have cum then probably orgasmed. I hated him at that moment. I called him a selfish pig, and then while in my rage and still shouting I knee'd him in his still erect penis.

As soon as I did it I felt so bad, he crumpled up and called me a "crazy bitch", we didn't even finish having sex. I still feel bad when I think back to it.

- **And then you have Whitney**

    Whitney was not always borderline crazy: She was actually quite normal when I first met her and we started dating. She still is at times and then the other times she's psycho.

Whitney is a new kind of crazy. Imagine what she would do if she found out about how I once felt about Leyton. **If she knew I would be eating more than dog food and probably suffering from a severe bout s of blue balls.** *Though, for a while I thought she knew due to the way she was acting.* I haven't made it obvious, I hope and have tried to be real careful as sometimes Whitney says and does stuff that makes me wonder if I'm safe about her.

She once gave me the dog's food in the form of lasagne (my favourite) for dinner after I commented on how bad her mums' cooking is.

I ate it all up, till she told me what she'd done and showed me the empty dog food packages in the trash.

Last Christmas I bought myself an iPad, as my own personal present. But after an argument on which relatives house we were going to spend Christmas day at (*which was obviously mine as her mother couldn't cook... and her dad keeps talking about marriage*), she stomped all over the iPad that I had only owned for a week and laughed in my face.

Whitney and I used to go out with my friends, on dates and on short weekend getaways. But now, nearly three years in and to ask Whitney to go to the pictures with me is like asking her to gouge out her eyes. She acts like you've offended her sensibilities. But when it's her asking me to go over to her mum's on a Sunday for lunch (when I should rightly be having sex with her), *I have no choice.*

I should have a choice, which would rightly be sexing her than eating or looking at her mother's offensive cooking.

Whitney knows how to get her way, typical of co-dependent Independent women. She sometimes likes to bargain with me: I go with her to her mums and she would go and watch a horror flick with me or whatever I have planned. I can't for the life of me count how many times I have gotten my request or deal out of the bargain. The only time would have been the first time we had made the bargain. After that she wouldn't uphold her end of the deal. Instead she would find a new way to make sure that I would go to her mums with her without doing my deal.

Whitney and I have been together now for some years, not a long time but long enough to be able to define her as an Emotional Co-Dependent Independent female. Truth be told as freaky as she is she scares me at times. The dog food incident is one of her less funky antics.

- ### Sex Kittens and the Freakish

   Sexy time with these women is another story compared to their moods.

   Can we say freaks in the house!

   The Emotionally Co-Dependent Independent women are very sexually open though not necessarily promiscuous **BUT** very adventurous none the less.

   Following?

   These women do not mind trying things out at least once say it be different sexual positions, to places and times to having sex. These are the women who when the opportunity to have sex presents itself while at the cinemas you can expect them in women's toilets going at it with their respective partner (*even in the back seats going at it- as Whitney likes*). These women will always have stories of the craziest places that *they have had sex.*

Diana 32 says;

The craziest place was in a children's play centre, with this cute guy that I met who worked there. I had acted as a chaperon for a trip there for my brother's class and this cute guy spent the whole day trying to spin a line on me. He succeeded and when we got back, I pulled him into a broom cupboard and rode him till I found my release.

Gene said;

I can beat that Diana. Try a park, in the middle of the day with a train packed full of people going past. I think that afternoon I got the best sex of my life as it was all the adrenaline and rush of probably getting caught.

Keaton 39

On the bus: Before I met my husband I was with my then boyfriend Dean, we were on our way home. Am guessing what we were doing beforehand must have left us a bit frisky or in the mood. I can't remember what bus it was on but, it was night time and we were the only ones on the top bunk of the bus. We were talking one minute, then we started kissing and God knows what happened as all I remember was straddling him and he whispering sweet nothings in my ear while I cam all over his lap. I still blush anytime I get on a bus.

Warren .N 24

My girlfriend Sally once surprised me at work while I was closing up the shop. I had let my staff leave early while I finished off some paper work, so we where both alone. She was sitting on the chair opposite my desk, watching me. I remember that she slowly removed her jacket and was wearing a tight black dress. I got so turned on, as she was looking at me and peeling off the dress. I had my eyes glued as she walked around the desk, got onto her knees and well.... you can guess the rest. That was the first time she'd ever done something like that, and to be honest I loved it. I always welcome her spontaneousity within our sex life. I take all her shit just for the sex. It's the best at all times.

@Bertha.net wrote;

I have been married for nearly 20 years and have found that keeping my husband always guessing sexually keeps our marriage evolving. I have made him watch me while I pleasured myself, and I have in turn made him masturbate in front of me while I watch and when his about to buss I go south and suck every last bit of his spunk. I find it sexy.

Dee 29,

Do I have to mention the restaurant? No, Okay... I gave my boyfriend a hand job while we were eating dinner with some of our closest friends. It was funny. We were all talking and catching up, he was sitting next to me and I thought what the hell. He was so shocked and surprised, he couldn't speak properly. I would ask him questions to put him on the spot- I never knew he stuttered: When he was about to cum his face crumpled up and his body jerked. They all looked at him and were asking him 'if he was ok'. It was really hard to look at him with a straight face; he hasn't forgiven me yet for that.

Gerry A states;

I was on a long hull flight with my girlfriend to New Zealand from the States for a two week holiday. They turned the cabin lights off and everyone seemed to be sleeping. She sat on my lap face forward and you can guess what happened.

Sexually experimentative and very open to new experiences. I love these women!

Whitney once took off her thong while we were driving and masturbated with her fingers. I parked the car up and helped her finish off. Whitney maybe crazy but at times the things she does drives me into Boner-Ville City. Some days I am a constant visitor!

But fair warning these women know the game, they know how to use sex to get what they want.

Zara G 29

'I think its obvious what men respond to and how I can get what I need from them. Sex is the answer to all my problems. I have no problem using sex to twist my boyfriends into submission. If I want that designer purse then I **teach** him in the bedroom.

Tarisha 40

I maxed out, I mean seriously maxed out our joint account while on a shopping trip with the girls. I just got promoted at work and though it was time for a total imagine upgrade to go with my new position. When he got back from work that day and for the rest of the month I gave him more than the normal performance in bed. Even let him do his favourites. I tried to repay the money but it was impossible, so by the time he got the statement, he was too tired to deal with it.

> Man the power of what's between a woman's thighs is powerful. They say that sex sells but I think their wrong, Sex is power and women have all of it as much as I hate to say.

Whitney decided that she wanted in and filled out part of a questionnaire....

'Two months into Troy and I dating I was involved in a minor fender bender which meant that my car was in the shops for a while. (It wasn't my fault as the other driver should have known that I was turning even though my indicators were not on. It was implied through my actions and the position of the car)

Troy took it upon himself to pick and drop me off at work when he could which I thought was really sweet. But then when I would ask to use his car, (instead of him constantly acting as my driver) he would always say something like- **'NO, you're not allowed to drive my car'.... 'Look at what you did to your car'... 'You're like a hazard on the road.'**

He went on like this for a week, and the day before I was getting my car from the shops, I decided it was about time I drove his car plus I had some errands to run, so I took his keys while he was out with a few friends.

I was driving down the main road and about to turn into another road when some crazy ass driver came out of nowhere and clipped the back of his car. It wasn't my fault as I was turning and the other guy clipped me. It's like no one knows how to drive properly or at least reasonably. I didn't call Troy straight away as I wanted to finish running my errands and thought he wouldn't be back home too soon. **Unfortunately for me, when I got back to his house he was already there with his friends. He was pissed would be an understatement. He threw a hissing fit which I thought was unreasonable about his car... He didn't even care that I could have suffered some sort of injury. He wasn't speaking to me, or answering my calls or texts: After a week of being dodged and ignored I turned up at his door step in a trench. As soon as he opened his door, I barged my way through, walked into the living and dropped the coat. I think that cheered him up as we were back on after that.... "**

What can I say- other than I am a red blooded male and she was naked!!!

- Partners

To be honest this group has had me for a pickle. Before reading the comments and talking to these ladies, I had the idea that the type of men/ partners they would go for would be a total mesh between the two groups: So he would have some similarities to you, with regards to background, knowledge and maybe wealth. And he would also be of no distinct type and subjected to no lists and be bullshit free.

Well was I wrong. It seems that these women are all over the place. As in - they have no distinct partner types.

It's all about whoever fits the bill at that point.

Partners are partners for these women; they can be as similar or as different to them as no care and emphasis is put on this by them.

6. An Interruption to THE SCHEDULE

Matt and Whitney decided to surprise me for my birthday and take me on a surprise two week "couples" cruise to the Bahamas. Two weeks for which my feelings rekindled and fizzled out indefinitely for Leyton. Two weeks of drama intense eye opening nonsense and two weeks for which my friendship and respect for Matt peaked faltered and reached an all time WTF scenarios.

For a while prior to the trip Matt had been saying that we should go on holiday like we used to do with the guys before Leyton or Whit came along. I would always say 'sure, why not.... but for now, with all my deadlines at work- I can't do it.'

He probably got tired of my excuses... So he went behind mu back to Whit, bribed her or begged then got her onboard behind my back **not** for the sole purpose of a birthday gift or a surprise for me, **but** so that he could get back in Leyton's good graces. *The little shit!*

As ever, since the baby incident Matt has really been trying hard to smooth things over with Leyton by buying her gifts, showering her with false affections and taking her on mini breaks: *The weekend following the big revelation of Shai and the baby, Matt took Leyton on a "bonding weekend" to Italy. Two weeks later it was an "I'm trying here, please forgive me as I know I made a big mistake" weekend trip to Paris. And shortly before the cruise, Matt whisked Leyton on a "let's start a family trip"* to Chicago (and also so Leyton could visit her family).

With Leyton, all Matt's gimmicks have worked. All the trips and gifts where just added bonuses for her as, when Matt initially apologised the night that Leyton found out about Shai and the baby, that was it and they were back on track like nothing ever happened in Leyton's eyes. She even laughs off the cheating and this baby situation as *"Matt's indiscretion"*.

If I ever pulled that stunt with Whit, I would be castrated and de-skinned within an inch of my life. And as crazy as that sounds, I respect that as Whitney wouldn't put up with such disrespectful actions as me cheating and acting a fool on her.

But that aside, the trip was needed, including all the hang-ups and drama that followed it. So to say, it opened my eyes in more than many ways; Matt is a prick but still my guy, Leyton an idiot and I'm totally over that and Whit, well she is still the same and we are still in our mindless relationship- craziness and all.

**

The trip started off alright, actually, better than alright- It started off great; with us all going out and enjoying what was offered on and off the cruise ship. We visited the local islands, even snorkelled and jet skied. I even found out that Whitney has an irrational fear of snorkelling, which was funny as she didn't mind swimming while we were on the beaches or even in the pool.

The second week started off slow, but picked up when Matt decided to bring out his inner whorish behaviour and sleep with a newlywed bride on her honeymoon which of course caused a fight between Matt and the bride's husband when he discovered them in a life raft going at it (they were pretty loud and could be heard some distance away from the life rafts). *They drew a crowd because of how loud they were in the first place and therefore how the groom found his bride in the compromising situation.*

Leyton, Whitney and I were on the other side of the deck when the whole commotion started. We heard and saw staff attendants and other holiday goers rushing towards the spot and decided to go and see what was going on. When we walked up to see what the commotion was, the bride was attempting to retie her bikini top while crying and apologizing to her husband who was trying beat all the senses out of Matt. Matt was laughing which obviously incensed the groom further and made the bride cry louder. The crowd was jeering when the groom landed his first punch to Matt face- even I laughed as he deserved it.

Leyton on the other hand did her usual and ran off crying. I told Whitney to go after her and I 'would sort out the situation'.

It took me and another 5 other guys including 3 staff members to drag and hold back the groom off a laughing Matt who emerged with a torn shirt and a cut above his left eye.

I should have left Matt to it as I got punched in the eye and my shirt ripped just for helping him. He found it funny and thought it was wise to taunt the groom who was still being held back by at least 6 different people telling the groom that he *'wasn't finished with his bride yet and would give her a good fucking before he got off board.'*

Before the groom could react anymore I pulled Matt through an entry way and walked him in the direction of our rooms.

I was so pissed that I couldn't talk. My eye was stinging and Matt was still laughing at the situation. We walked back to the rooms in silence where Leyton and Whitney were waiting for us. By the time we entered Leyton was still in floods of tears while Whit was trying to calm her down.

'Hey baby, what's the tears for', where Matt's first words.

'What the fuck Matt, seriously you couldn't act right for another couple of days?' Whitney was shouting, she looked fuming- more so than Leyton did. *'What the fuck is wrong with you!'* She finished

At this point all Leyton is doing is looking up at Matt, still crying and as each minute rolls ion she becomes louder and more hysterical. *Just when I was wishing she would shut the hell up she runs into the on-suite bathroom and locks herself in.*

'Whit, what's your problem? I was just having a bit of fun... And she came onto me, not the other way.' Matt said with a smirk on his face.

'You where just caught shagging another woman, who's not Leyton... that's not having a bit of fun. That's taking the fucking piss. And being damn disrespectful to all parties involved.' Whit looks at me points and says *'You should have let the guy beat the living shit outta him.'* She looks back at Matt and says

'...as you sure as hell deserve it.'

Ignoring Whitney, Matt walks over to the on suite, knocks on thee and tells Leyton to *'open the door'*, which she does.

At this point am done, I ask Leyton if she is ok, which she replies with a nod, and says *'Thanks Troy, can you guys give us a min.'*

'Sure', I said and got Whitney who I had to practically drag out their room and into ours.

Whatever happened and was said seemed to do the trick, as that evening when we all met for dinner, Leyton and Matt where acting like a newlywed couple. From that point on the rest of the week was tension filled, and awkward with Whitney acting hostile to both Leyton (for allowing Matt to get away with his shenanigans') and Matt (for being disrespectful to Leyton who didn't seem to think anything of his reactions).

**

I guess actually being there and witnessing the cheating, Leyton's crying and then some words spat out by Matt, then the makeup leaves me thinking otherwise and feeling indifferently to Leyton and somewhat of Matt. I have known Matt and his family since childhood so regardless of how I have felt about Leyton nothing will break our friendship (though he nor Leyton will not be hearing anytime soon from me as I need a rest from all the drama). Leyton now and foremost for me will be considered as my best friends girlfriend, and my girlfriends friend- that's it. She (Leyton) may look great in a bikini and be nice to talk to but she is too emotionally needy and willing to be in a dysfunctional relationship just to be in a relationship. (Does the term emotional dependent ring a bell?)

I think little of Leyton since then, I feel that she obviously thinks so low of herself and is cool with Matt's antics and loves him more than enough to tolerate his cheating and constant disrespect of her. Matt has her wrapped around his fingers, toes and words. Who am I to judge him on that, I should applaud him- I wish sometimes that I could have that manipulation thing down so that I too can have Whitney under some sort of control. If only!

7. The Miscellaneous OTHERS.

Mandy B wrote;

'I cooked his denture in my piss and put it back in his sterilizing holder (without the sterilizing liquid) ready for him to insert it into his dirty ass mouth. He cheated on me and gave me Chlamydia so I thought it was only good of me to repay him back by pissing and rubbing my Chlamydia soaked vagina in what he put in his mouth.'

Rosie stated;

After a night out with the girls, I had a dare I had to perform... So the next morning, I woke my boyfriend up to hot wax pouring on his inner thighs and accidentally on his testicles... He screamed and cried "Bloody Mary"... While kicking me off the bed, I was laughing so hard that I pee'd my pants

Telling him was it was a dare was unimaginable to him.

It took him a while to forgive me. That week he hobbled everywhere, it was funny to watch. He still has a small scar from the hot wax on his inner thigh, but in defense- It was a dare and I don't renege on dares!

Even now when I think we should be laughing about it (as I always am) he gets all mad and calls me a crazed Bitch and skulks off in a mood.

Devlin 26 said

'I told my ex that I wasn't ready to have kids.... any time soon with him. [As after] looking at a few baby pictures of him and his brother, and his brother's kids- I thought that the kids I would have with him would be too ugly to look at.

It's bad enough that anytime his brother brings his kids around I have to smile and say how "cute" his ugly kids are. **It's like they all have overly large alien looking heads with buck tooth's coming out of their mouths. Their mother smiles with all her teeth pointing out at you- imagine that, it's terrifying.**

I can't imagine pushing one of them out of me.... and **I don't want to cringe and cry anytime I look at my baby.'**

These three lovely ladies are just the tip of an ever so interesting iceberg.

We shall take a quick break here and go to the more scientific explanation for these subsidiaries' and more.

Previously, you have heard me mention that there are a number of subsidiaries within the main three categories. So far I have introduced you to two of the main subsidiaries; Emotionally Co-Dependent Dependents and the Emotionally Co- Dependent Independents.

So to aide me further in explaining these other subsidiaries from the three main groups that have yet to be discussed I have to explain how I came about them. So am going to use my human science/ behavioural sciences background to further explain...

***Warning it will get technical ***

After I collated all the materials used to gather my information from my interviews, public discussions, surveys/questionnaires etc, with the female and male participants: they were then grouped into three main categories; the emotional dependents, the emotional co-dependents and the emotional independent females.

The females categorised as emotionally co-dependent were further divided into three separate groups after close examination of some of their responses: The Emotionally Co- Dependent was the figure head or umbrella for which the Emotionally Co-Dependent Dependents and the Emotionally Co- Dependent Independent branched from.

The same divisions occurred with both the Emotionally Dependent and the Emotionally Independent females as after putting the responses for each category into separate piles, inputting the collected data and using a systematic coded approach the results from several tests performed showed some statistical outliers.

(That was a mouthful!)

These outliers naturally were far from the rest of the data but similar in some ways, so- they could not be placed into one of the three main categories. After close examination of the data and corresponding collated material I found that as the material which resulted in the outliers varied ever so slightly from their main counterparts that they created a new sub categorized category. They therefore had no basis in any of the groups and subsidiaries discussed already.

(Another mouthful)

As they had no basis in any of our already established categories due to their non conformist responses I decided it was best that I introduce you to them and we discuss these responses further.

But please note:

Though, I have named the subsidiaries of the Emotionally Co Dependent group, I have not named the subsidiaries of the Emotionally Dependent and Independent groups as they are much smaller (I'm not saying they are insignificant) but they have slight variations for which naming could cause some confusion.

*** We are back to normal broadcasting***

Now that was all tongue tying...

Time to lighten the mood and get down to the fun part:

- ### I'm Pregnant!!!

Okay, so I thought this only happened in soaps and soap operas, where the female lead pretends to be pregnant to keep the guy?

But was I wrong! I posed a question- deceivingly as I expected all participants to veer towards the latter of the question.

'Have you ever at any point in any relationship lied to your partner about your health, financial wealth or family?'

A clear majority of my respondents stated that they had lied about their finances which I thought was a normal occurrence since I had done that in the past to several of the women I had dated as I didn't want to spend money on them. A handful of participants actually admitted to lying about the family and family background. But my outliers came from two female participants.... two very interesting participants:

Natalie H 32 stated

We were going through a rough patch in our marriage and he kept talking about wanting to leave. I was late and well was sure that I was pregnant, so I told him... Unfortunately for me I wasn't as my period came a week later. I didn't tell him as we started to bond more and we were just like we were when we first got married. We were happy again and started to have sex more.

I hid my period from him the first month but then the second month I woke up and it was there... He saw the blood on the bed and thought I was having a miscarriage and started to panic. I tried to calm him down and tell him it was normal but he had me in the car and on the way to the ER before I knew it.

The doctor broke the news to him... that it was just my period and gave me a pad.

I silently got dressed as he sat there in tears. I felt so bad that I told him the truth. He left me at the hospital and by the time I got home he had packed his things and left.

Doreen stated

I have told loads of white lies.... It's a healthy and normal thing to do. I told my boyfriend that I was pregnant and would only keep the baby if we got married. He proposed shortly after and we broke the engagement news to all our families and friends.

When we went to the Doctor's for a check-up, the Doctor broke the news that I wasn't pregnant while my fiancé comforted a crying me and telling me that he loved me and still wanted to marry me. (That helped me cry for real)

The Doctor told us that sometimes pregnancy tests can sometimes show a false positive due to several things and that's what happened in our case.

We got married the following year and to this day he has no clue of my treachery.

Happy news... I AM FOUR MONTHS PREGNANT NOW with our first child.

Imagine a scale- on emotions based on the three main groups we have discussed including the two subsidiaries.

Pictured it yet?

Well, these women would be between the Emotional Dependent AND Emotional Co-Dependent categories. This is due to their use of manipulation to keep that dying relationship afloat.

These women have more Emotional Dependent traits and would be classified as dependents **but for** their manipulation and lying in those instances. However, it should be noted that these women would fit in **somewhat** with the Co- Dependent Independents category, but then due to their diehard **need** of being in **that** relationship (see Natalie and Doreen's statements again) they would fall short on other aspects of the Co-Dependents and Co-Dependent Independent females.

These women have been driven to the extreme due to the over powering need of the relationship which is why they report as outliers of the Emotional dependents.

- ~~**The psychotic ones**~~ **WTF**

I think out of all the groups and subsidiaries, these women freak me out the most. As they have no care.

These women can make the Emotionally Independent females blush.... and put the Emotional Dependents in tears. I laughed out loud when I read some of the responses written. Some of these ladies are unique, to put correctly- they're different.
Their responses leave you thinking- "bitch" to 'is she ok....seriously, what's wrong with her.'

I thought Whitney was crazy, and borderline. But these women take the biscuit.

They are the women more likely to take the low road and really teach you about a woman's scorn.

They don't look or act as crazy as can be till shit hits the fan and you push that button.

I don't know where to begin, or even what else to say for these few...

Their motto... 'Don't fuck with me, unless you can handle what happens.'

Mark ****@****.com wrote in;

My babies mother apparently found out that I had been cheating on her the day before my 21st birthday party. So she made me a "special" birthday cake full of shit for me.

Yes, she actually made a cake of shit.... poop for me.... as a birthday cake.

I don't know how she found out, but she did.

Before the actual cutting of my cake, she made a special announcement and brought out the cake in front of all the guests... She cut a slice of the cake which smelt foul up close and threw it at me. IT hit the side of my face and I was pissed but [bleep] that [bleep] is crazy. She started shouting at me and told me that she knew about my cheating. It took four of my boys to hold her back.

She's only 5ft 3 and about 110 pounds, and it was easy holding her back.

We haven't talked since then.... She's crazy and I have a restraining order against her.

Santana B from West midlands wrote;

..... I once mixed cayenne pepper with lube and used it to give my boyfriend a hand job. I made sure that my hand went everywhere around and on his dick so that no area was missed, including the head of his dick.

By the time I was done, he was in pain, and I didn't care. I told him what I DID WHILE HE STUCK HIS SWOLLEN DICK IN COLD WATER. He drove himself to the ER in pain.

That taught him never to give me an STI or cheat on me again.

> → Does it say something about me if I would rather Whitney's dog food Lasagne antics over any of what these women have cooking up their revenge filled minds.

@Tina***.net wrote

While my ex slept, I emptied out a small tube of 'Super Super Glue' on his junk and used a pen to try and get his penis stuck to his balls... While doing this he started to stir, so I stopped and tried to get the pen before he woke up.

It was stuck, and very fast acting!

He didn't wake up but turned over. I wrote him a message to tell him that we were done and used Super Super Glue to stick it to his bare hairy [arse].

I hoped he enjoyed my present!!

I hope he ripped his skin while trying to unglue his junk- the prick.

> I wonder what he did to get that: That sounds painful. These women are heartless. They **would** fit right in with the Emotional Independent females but they have one screw too loose for the opportunistic Independents.
>
> These women are on the outskirts and sitting on the fence to another group outside of the Independents. *I would say* ***they are the extremist of the extremists.***

- **And then you have**

To be honest I don't understand these ones...

On an Emotional scale these women would likely fit into the Emotionally Co-Dependent Independent crazies, but not totally due to some of their more out there actions.

Their attitudes are blasé and very different- at best.

Mrs. A for anonymous wrote;

I once woke up so horny after an interesting dream, that I turned over and started jerking my boyfriend off. I got even more aroused the harder he got and couldn't take it any longer. So I sat on his face.

He started going to work on me while I was sucking him off; he stopped suddenly and told me to get off of him (in not so nice words). That's when I saw the blood all over his face and a sodden tampon just between his lips.

Shit! I totally forgot I was on my period. The dream was that good!

I couldn't help but laugh while he freaked out.

He thought I had done it on purpose... Whatever... I kept laughing and told him to calm the fuck down and that it was just a little bit of blood and that he should stick a condom on so we could finish off.

I mean a little bit of blood is nothing, I work in an ER and have seen worse!!

<u>Incognito who? Wrote;</u>

'I was seeing this chick, who thought it would be sexy to send me a video of her getting her p***y pierced.

It was disgusting, there was blood there and I could hear her letting out a squeal when the guy got piercing.

I would have rather a sexy lingerie shot of her... What made her think that that video was a good idea, let alone a sexy one at that?'

Terry C 39 said;

'My friend has got amazing hair. It's silky, strong, and long and thick. I asked her what she used on her hair to make it like that... She said that she drinks (swallows after oral) and rubs her husband's spunk on her hair. She said that her "doctor" even said it was good for her because of some nutrients it carries.

I tried rubbing some of my boyfriends on my hair.... and well I didn't find out whether to wash it off and ended up going to work with patches of my hair caked in spunk. I didn't notice the difference after a week of doing it.... and my boyfriend refused to sleep with me till I washed all the spunk off my hair.

He said it was gross.'

- **The Unusual Breakup Artists**

    Breakups are sensitive matters and for any of the Emotional categories regardless of which end of the break up stick they're on, these women understand the sensitivity of breaking up.

So when it comes to breaking up with their respective partners- the Emotionally Dependents, *(the ones that are used to being on the receiving end of a break up- they're the ones more likely to be dump),* the Emotionally Co-Dependents and their subsidiaries *(who are used to both being the dumpee and the dumper)* and the Emotionally Independent females *(the expert breakup artists)* understand that drawing attention whether wanted or unwanted could cause embarrassment on their parts if they publicise the break up and its reasons.

Our outliers on the other hand, these ladies as you will read, don't care about drawing the attention to their breakups. As for them- all they care about is the **revenge factor**; thereby the more public and humiliating the revenge is, the better and sweeter it is for these women. **But For** these actions of these ladies they would fit nicely within either the Emotionally Independent or Co-Dependent Independent groups.

Remember: It's all about the dumpee's feeling worthless for the Emotional Co-Dependent Independents' and the Emotionally Independents'.

Natalie 45 states

'I bought space in my local newspaper and in several out there magazines advertising my ex as a male gigolo with his picture and details. It wasn't a small space either.

I bet he got loads of unwanted callers.

I made sure that I plastered a few of the adverts cut into flyer in the phone booths and local pubs in and around our area.'

A very angry ex states;

'My wife of 6 years decided it was clever to announce to all and whoever was listening at the time via live radio that she wanted a divorce, she put me on blast and made some not so nice comments about me. She even questioned my sexuality, by making some farfetched comments that had my mother calling me to ask me whether I was gay. Some of my friends, work colleagues and family heard it and called me while it was being aired. To make matters worse it was played over and over again throughout the day and was used as news feed.

I live in a small town so, by the end of that day everyone had heard about and I was the new laughing stock of the town.

Two weeks after the incident the radio was still playing parts of it. I had to threaten them with a lawsuit before they took it off their webpage and stopped airing it as sound bites.

It was embarrassing, still is. Six months after the incident and I am still the laughing stock of my town.

Tracy B 38

My boyfriend of 8 years said that he felt that I had emasculated him so he couldn't be with me anymore. I was baffled to what he meant so I sent out an email using his email address, addressed to me- so it looked like he was sending a sexy email to me: In the send to box I highlighted all his contact from work and personal.

The email consisted of a picture of him naked... with an itty bitty penis. (I had photo shopped a naked picture of him that he had sent to me a while back)

The subject line read.... 'Hey babe this is for deserts...'

It was too funny...

Rita 51 stated;

My husband went through what he liked to call a mid life crisis and had an affair of ten years and had two kids and expecting a third with the woman. He told me about it the night before our 30 year anniversary as he felt too guilty and wanted it all out.

He said he loved me and couldn't explain his actions... My response was actually, 'okay, I understand. So what do you want me to do about it?'

I was numb, and didn't say much after that.

The day of the party, it was like I was on auto pilot. I packed most his clothes and things into two large black trash bags and put them in the down stairs coat closet.

When all our friends, family, kids and grand children arrived- I smiled and played hostess till it was time for the speeches.

Gone was my speech on how thankful I was to have met a man like Jerome that I loved and who loved me. Gone was me thanking him for 30 years of wedded bliss. I didn't care about that anymore.

So I said... 'I will like all of you to follow me outside as I have a surprise for Jerome.'

I grabbed my son's baseball bat from the coat closet as everyone filed out of the house to see the big surprise. As they all stood watching, I walked over to Jerome's car, smiled, pitched my hand with the bat and swung smashing his driver window. It felt good... and everyone including Jerome stood in shock watching me. I swung and hit a couple more times breaking the windscreen, driver and signal lights.

I paused for a second to catch my breath and addressed a bewildered Jerome and party guess;

'I will be divorcing Jerome since he saw it fit to have a mistress for 10 years of our 30 year marriage, with whom he has two kids with and another on the way.'

At this point my oldest son asked his father if it was true. Jerome stood there with his head down, before saying, as if he thought it would make everything different told me that '[he] was sorry and still loves me and that I can't just throw away 30 years of marriage.'

I looked at him and let out a cackle;

'Jerome I have packed what I can of yours in the black trash bags I left in the coat closet, I want to get them and leave now, FYI I emptied out our "nest egg".'

A few more hits with the bat and I was done... Everyone and my sons stood there transfixed, Jerome was blubbering about the car and nest egg...

I didn't care anymore- 'The party is over, please all get your coats and go.... Oh and thank you all for your gifts again,' was all I managed to them.

After I got rid of everyone from the house, I got out my camera and took photos of the rest of Jerome's things and put them on eBay.

Kristie stated;

My boyfriend told me he loved me a week back, after 9 months of us dating.

I replied by smiling at him then saying; 'that's nice but love is an overrated feeling which you put too much value on.' I haven't heard from him since.... and I have tried to call him- even leaving texts and email messages for him.

I guess another one bites the dust.

***

The last guy that Whitney dated before we got together still calls begging to get back with her. I ask her what happened... She just says she dumped him and then gets all cryptic and coded about what exactly happened.

8. SO What Does THIS ALL MEAN?

Natalie B 21 stated;

'Is this for real?

Man! My older sister sounds like a Co- Dependent Independent.

She's crazy like that. This woman Whitney has nothing on my sister.

She once put a snake in her boyfriend's car after they had had a blow up. You should have interviewed her- she's loco. Her last boyfriend dumped her after she left two dead rats in his bed. Apparently he had cheated on her and when she found out, she had left the rats there as a symbol of his "rat like ways"- I guess.

I think that this is interesting... Do you mean that you men really see us like this?

This sucks... As I would say that I'm a Co-Dependent Dependent. As I so fit the profile.

Did I mention that this sucks!'

- **So what, what does all this mean? What's he trying to say? What does he know?**

Are these the questions you're asking yourselves?

I asked myself the same questions and others have asked me the same questions and to be truthful I had no perfect answer that came to mind, except that as a man writing and researching about women and women's emotions in relationships is always controversial- *As, what do men know about being a woman- right?*

Well I find myself up for the challenge, the disdain and general critics that may arise from this whole experience.

This whole episode started off as a rant (on women who I found frustrating after they dealt with the same problems that others go through in irrationally irritating ways than others) which led down the path of personal discovery of enlightenment that I wished to share with others hence this read.

- ## *Addressing some of the general critics!!*

At no point did I seek to turn this read into a self help book as I have been brandished and criticized about:

When I initially started this explorative rant, I only sought to shine some sort of light into what I found, into what I perceived and attributed from what I interpreted of my findings to mean. It may have come off **'frank and direct and sometimes rude'** but take as you want from it as I give no apologises for being truthful and to the point of what my finding where and interpreted as.

At the time I wrote and was writing the first chapter or first few pages that turned into a chapter, I was feeling exasperated from all the Leyton, Matt and Whitney issues and the fact that others where bombarding me with their own personal problems and expecting me to give them the right answer or advice. I was frustrated and got my trusted laptop out and started typing. I typed that first chapter without some of the contributing outsiders such as *Tram or Paula*. I didn't want to change the first few pages that consisted of a chapter as I felt that they reflected my state of mind and it also kept within the spirit of the read, my thought processes at the time and how I felt. I wanted those who read this to get an unambiguous insight to my feeling and attitude to such topics and discussions and thought processes at the time.

Some comments have been that the first chapter may comes off incoherent and if that is so I do suggest that you re-read it again and maybe you will understand what I was getting at.

I am not apologetic that some might find that I come across pompous and or obnoxious, as that is how you have interpreted it. I did not purposely try and throw my smarts at you unfortunately this is how you took it. Maybe I should take lessons in *how to address myself in more likeable terms and less outspoken ways when writing* but what the hell I haven't. I like my grittier more outspoken way with words.

One individual asked whether I got consent about using identifying names and details. My response was:

Please understand I am not green in conducting or performing research so I know and understand that research 101 or ethics 101 is getting consent from participants and letting them know what is to be done with the material, data and findings. I was given consent by all of those who participated through the different means and they were aware that just for added precautious their identities who remain anonymous as I would change any identifiers which I did.

'... Because of your hatred for self help books and the like you are unlikely to get help or advice on the book or even a publishing deal as this could affect their sales/image/branding in the long run if the climate favours self help books and they go in that direction as a result of publishing yours.'

I may have come off too strong on my dislike on self help books, but that is how I feel. Self help books dictate **what you should and shouldn't do.** My read address my observation and at no point does it say **you must do this to get laid or do that to stop being treated as this....** All it does is make frank observations as to my findings and interpretation. You personally may feel that this read instructs the readers to turn into Emotional Co-Dependents but that is your assumption and what you have interpreted this read to be.

I repeat, **this is no self help book, it is a book based on observation and public personal experiences on a subject matter that was initially based on frustration and a yearning to understand using research as a tool to this process.**

'... I would consider re-writing [the first chapter and maybe more and] being more tactful in communication. I have found people tend to buy based on the person not the product. If they don't like the person it doesn't matter how good a product is their sales will be limited. Just a few points to consider...'

Thank you again for your insight. Duly noted and appreciated. I have taken what you said into consideration and find that I do not write my research for popularity, fame and or monetary purposes (though all are welcome- *smile, wink and nod*). So if I was to do as you suggest I would feel that I am giving my readers an edited and less viable piece of reading material which then devalues my work. I understand that **you** feel the need to *pull the wool over anyone's eyes* to make yourself more marketable- I totally get that, but I do not operate in the same way. I do not task myself with that duty lying or making sure that everyone has the truth... I just make sure that when I speak, I speak what I know and make sure it is right so that I do not put in correct information out in circulation. **But I thought I was being tactful? Wasn't I?**

- **Let the good times keep rolling??**

Mr. ANNOYMOUS stated

'... This means that we men put up with too many emotional spurts from women. It means that Troy has found a helping for us men. Now I know which type of women I like.... The Emotional Co-Dependent Independents as you said they were crazy in bed.... that's a turn on and no wonder Troy is with Whitney.

If you ever get tired of her I will gladly take her off your hands.'

@Flora*** WROTE**

'I think that from what this guy writes he has picked up on the dim-witted sense that some women display in relationships.... I mean, just the other day I witnessed my niece- a smart and loving no nonsense girl- allow her boyfriend to disrespect her in *front of me. I don't know what happened or why they were arguing but he called her a bitch and a worthless whore.*

That is not on, and I don't tolerate such language to anyone. I couldn't stand for it and had to tell him off and to watch his tongue before I marched him off my property.

She ran off crying after. It was disappointing to see and yet very worrying....

I think this guy Troy has something here and is speaking the truth... Though, I find that he maybe a little bit jaded after his experience with that Mrs. [Xxxx] lady.'

Pauline T wrote

This is ALL cock. What it means is that you have a problem with getting one woman though you already have a girlfriend- YOU RAT, so you decide to go on a one man crusade bashing us women and degrading our baser instincts.

Where do you get off from?

Kick sticks and don't quit your day job.

- **So what did you think about all of this**

   It was only fair that at the end of my findings and well this whole READ that gage others reactions to my observations as we have already been doing. So to see how others react to what is being said and possible implications- if any, I took samples of my findings, the examples and insightful giving's of those who participated in some way or another in this research and extended rant (whatever you want to call it) to see how the public would react.

Gerry 29 from LA wrote

As insightful as this read as you call it is- I feel that it is unfair and biased and moulds women into three categories that are extremes of the extremes. Your introduction and definition of the three categories and possible other miscellaneous categories are enlightening and insightful. But I find that some of the examples (the people you talked to where either stupid or stupider) and explanations are rather gauche representation of women.

If I had to pick I would be an Emotional Independent as I am no gold-digger but I do love my men to be light and giving with the money. I also find that I break up with partners as I am too picky... I only deserve the best and if you don't meet my criteria- then skip. I have no tolerance- you where right about that though!

Nope... am not going to retaliate and call Gerry or my other critics' degenerates.... That's rude- I hear!

There always has to be one or many. I will though thank you Gerry and the others for this insightful feedback...

Throughout this whole process I have interacted, interviewed, conversed and administered the survey questionnaires to a varied population from all walks of life and class and areas of the globe that I was able to interact with. I even interviewed, conversed while I travelled nationally and internationally, which meant that I got to interact with a wider response, and received responses with experiences and examples from different perspectives' and individuals which lends us a better more rounded insight, THEREFORE allowing me to generalize my views.

I do however apologize if you feel that I have over generalized, and put the "extremes of the extremes"- as you put it... But I only included what was submitted and stated.

Ms M stated

'You tell me [which group of women I would be in]!!

When it's my night away from my baby and husband; it's affair night for me. I take my ring off, rent a hotel room just to shower (so that I don't smell like baby or my house), redress and for whatever may happen afterwards.

So what group do you feel that makes me?

(I really hope it the crazy one.... the Emotionally Co- Dep Independents).

P.S I love your girlfriend Whitney. From what you have written and said of her, she's off the charts... Next time my hubby says something crazy or does something crazy- I may use the dog food casserole thing... That's classic.

"A" wrote;

I think I would get crucified by any of my friends or family if they know this. But I so agree with Leyton... And am sorry but Whitney seems like a bitch.

I've caught my husband cheating on me before- we are still together. He even had a child with the woman and I have welcomed my step son into my family. I love my husband, and find that due to how much I love him I can deal with all the other stresses that comes with maintaining a good relationship.

If understanding and thinking that Leyton has been right in standing by her man makes me an Emotional Dependent so be it.

No name wrote;

'Seriously women, these just shows us that WE DO put too much emphasis on that word LOVE and stay in NO GOOD relationships in the name of love. We get hurt and disrespected in the name of love. Cheating is cheating and once is way too much for my liking.

Interesting read and I would love to see the final version when you are done.'

Lupita M said

'I would consider myself to be in one of the subsidiary categories.... what you called "borderline cases" (BTW this is going to be my new term- "borderline case")

.... I love to publicise the breakup of a relationship. My ex's have called me a "show queen" as I love the lime light in which ever form I can get it. My ex broke up with me as he said I was too much drama for him to handle- so I got his Facebook, MySpace, Yahoo Messenger including email account hacked and a picture of him wearing my underwear posted on all walls- with a caption saying "and this is what you get for thinking you where better than me, Love LUPITA".

He called the cops... and now has a restraining order on me- but I don't think that it's needed as I'm so over him. I have a new boyfriend who hopefully won't fuck about with me and my feelings. '

NC wrote

I feel that Leyton was right by sticking with Matt but then I think she is too much of a push over. I can't say otherwise but yeah I would have too stuck by my man as everyone cheats at sometime. Right?

Cheating is not a big deal or a deal breaker as it once was deemed.

Relationships mean you have to deal with the good and bad, you just work through the cheating- it's another obstacle in the relationship.

Alana 23

'... Women are crazy, and I still don't get them. My girlfriend is too clingy and acts like I'm about to run away on her at all times. I think that's why she likes to handcuff me during sex....

She is one of those women that suffer from abandonment issues after her father ran out on her mother when she was a teen.'

Solo, A stated

'I love Mrs. X. She is my new hero and I think that we women should take a leaf out of her book. I would love to have that kind of arrangement with my husband and then sleep with and mind f**k another guy's brain- as guys do it to us women all the time.

It's time we do that to them, take back the power of our p***y.

P.S. Troy you so deserved what she did to you. You seem to be the biggest douche I have heard of. Whitney should leave you and find someone better.

(I hope you (Troy) weren't the one I talked to before filling this out as you where cute and I left my phone number on the back of my response sheet)'

Rhyana say's;

'It's funny and so true... It's what we all think but don't say. [We] women are complex creatures within and out of relationships- I have witnessed some of these traits you talk about and would not have thought to categorise as you did... I have to laugh....

But this is so cool and again so true.

What group? Maybe the Emotional Dependents as I have a tendency as you put it to cling- hang onto a disastrous relationship. I am currently in one.... and I don't know what I am doing.'

Tim 31 said

'.... I would say that my wife is an Emotional Co-Dependent Independent. Is that right, how you say it....? [As] she can act like a pit-bull at times! Arguing with her is another thing- you won't win- ever... I can never get a word in and if I try to say anything- she will shut it down. She once "accidently" poured hot wax on my bare chest. But I don't see how you could accidently pour hot wax. She is crazy and now I understand why.

Reading the definition of the emotional co-dependent independent females I think they are crazy... And that's my wife.

Karlie N stated;

'Leyton sounds like a turd. I can't stand women like that... My sister is like that.

I can't respect women who put themselves in nonsense situations like that. Women like that have no self respect or COMMON SENSE at all. If my boyfriend ever cheated and acted in such a way I wouldn't be with him.

That would be that.

I would be an Independent Soldier... But why do you make them sound so cold. Women of an Emotionally Independent nature are strong, proud and sexy. They know what they want and what they do not want. They do not demand respect, they get it.'

Becky wrote

'I don't want to think I am anyone of these categories except the Co-Dependents or Independents; but the category that closest fits me and I admittedly would put myself in is that of the Emotional Dependent females; as YES I LOVE RELATIONSHIPS AND WHAT THEY REPRESENT. Though I do not feel that I always have to be in a relationship... I just love being in a relationship and sometimes longer than needed. Yes, I haven't been the one to do the dumping... I am more the one to get dumped. Oh and I have done the booty call thing... but I was the one to get the call in the middle of the night from my ex.

My girlfriend of 2 years recently broke up with me. She said that I was too exhaustive to be with, and that she needed her space as she felt that I was suffocating her.

I don't understand what she meant by that as I did everything to please her- I would always make sure that I had cooked and cleaned for her, made sure that we spent as much time together... I even saw less of my family and friends just to spend more time with her.

My sister got married and I was meant to be the chief bridesmaid but when my ex got food poisoning and was laid up in bed I didn't leave her alone and had to miss my sister's wedding.

Tracy 52 stated

'Oh my God... I am so the EMPOWERING Emotionally Independent Female. I embrace who I am and do not TOLERATE NONESENE from ANYONE. Including my husband- the poor sap.

I agree as I for one look at other women who act so idiotic and "redonckulous" to their partner's stupid ways beneath me. I do not respect the Leyton's and the Emotionally Dependent and Emotionally Co- Dependent Dependents. They are cowards who do not know how to stand up for themselves and what is right.'

Rabi 28 wrote;

'Troy I don't know if you know this yet- BUT WHITNEY IS CRAZY.

Her crazy is not normal; I don't even think she is normal.

Am totally the opposite of her. I am caring and endearing to my partners. I love the obstacles' that comes with relationships. I have not been cheated on yet and hope not to face that. If ever that happened- I couldn't do what your girl Leyton did, as once is enough. If he is a persistent cheater then he obviously does not love you enough and you need to leave him.'

Shana said

'.... I think we should agree to disagree. You find my actions to be representative of being an Emotional Independent from our.... What ... 10 minutes conversation?

I find that highly judgmental and offensive: As from what you have said about these women they are bitches.

Do I look like a bitch? Better yet do not answer.'

'Shana, we have been talking for- yes 10 min, and at no point have I called you a bitch or labelled you as any of the categories. As I recalled I have just briefly outlined the three categories and what they are and represent... You haven't told me much about you and I judge not.' I said, taken aback by her whole explosion.

You would think that being with Whit makes me experienced in crazy... I see not!

Shana carries on;

Okay, well any-who... I see where you think you're coming from but men are a big cause for the way we women act in relationships. And we do not over emotionalize- you men just aren't in sync with your emotions so you make it a big issue when we show some emotion.'

Lance 45 wrote

This is interesting as I live in a house full of women. My wife would be a co-dependent and I hope my two girls take up the co-dependent traits when in a relationship.

I find that from what I have read of this Matt's character and his girlfriend Leyton- I could not in all my life respect such idiots. She's stupid for staying with him and he on the other hand has no respect for women to treat her that way. For her to allow it, shows there's a lot not right with her. If Leyton was one of my daughters I would lock her in a dark shed and beat the dumb attitude out of her. Matt I would run you over and then reverse over you.

Troy, man you're no better: That's your best friends girlfriend you where looking to hook up with.'

As you have read, the responses to this whole episode or my **"one man crusade on women and their emotions"** rant- as some would call it, have received very interesting and mixed responses.

Responses, that are valid and entertaining to hear- especially yours Lupita. *Seriously I am going to have to hide some of these responses from Whitney as I do not want her getting new ideas of even crazier antic to inflict on me. And Karlie I wished I had met you or your sister during my initial process and you Lupita as I would have loved to have interviewed and conversed with you.*

9. Whitney KNEW!

Two weeks after the cruise and all its interesting happenings, I woke up to Whitney watching me sleep. It was semi creepy but then her hands and mouth took a detour and woke my man up with a kiss and some oral worship. I was surprised... normally when I get such a gentle waking up like that; it's due to Whit doing or saying something that would cause some sort of argument. We didn't argue the night before? Nor do I remember her doing anything that would amount to her "making up" with me in such a way.

But I am not complaining- which sane person would (sometimes to get such treatment like that I would have to beg and probably eat her mother's poison). It was the best wake up I had had since we had been together... I loved every second of it- her mouth and tongue should be insured for more than J-Lo's assets.

That morning after all that, she made me breakfast which was great if Whitney was more culinary inclined. Whit can cook, she can (*I type this really trying to convince myself on this issue*) but with a very *very* limited cooking range; she can make a mean lasagne but at the same time can burn water (which as impossible as that is- Whitney can manage to do) and eggs which she did that morning.

I think it runs in her family as both her mother and sister act and cook "challenged" (why do you think I find it hard going there on a Sunday).

The breakfast was not what I was used to, the texture and taste of burnt eggs and bacon was interesting to say the least... *but I ate it as I liked that she wasn't in a crazy mood.* In fact since getting back from the cruise, Whitney had cooled down the crazy antics and we seemed to grow closer. The fact that I was out of lust with Leyton and hadn't really spoken to her since the cruise fiasco helped me concentrate on my relationship and Whitney. I had talked to Matt and we had gone out for a drink for a friend's birthday but I found that I was not interested anymore in his and Leyton's drama. I had my own to deal with.

I thought nothing of telling Whitney of my once lust filled designs on Leyton as that would cause unnecessary problems between me and her and it also would be a stupid idea as it no longer was important. *So you can imagine my face when Whit brought it up.*

Yes my mouth was agape!!

Her words... 'You're too cute... The way you would chase after Leyton when she would call you crying...'

I looked up at her, mouth open with a question mark over my head. *Pretend you know nothing and that she's winding you up,* was all that went through my thoughts. *Look blank and make sure that your eyes don't bulge out your head- remember denial is your "bf and lover".*

'...what you on about,' was all I could manage.

'Did you really think that I couldn't see through your love sick puppy dog act? I thought it was funny and sweet at first how you treated Leyton... Then it became a little pathetic, the way she would call you and then you would go running to her. Regardless what time and what you were doing, you would go running... I mean, I had no problem as I knew she wasn't going to sleep with you or notice how love sick you where acting.... Like, did you

really think that she was at any point in life going to break up with Matt, did you? Really! Any time soon.... Matt could give her genital warts or even Syphilis of the brains and Leyton would still be his lapdog. Women like that have to be kicked to the curb before they look at anyone else.'

She took a deep breath, and I stared on in complete wonder. Why was it that I didn't mind her confronting me, the more she got angry and exasperated the more turned on I got by the heat she was exuding. I had a hard on just watching her talking at me, she seemed really pissed. But why was she pissed that- I fancied Leyton- nothing ever did happen.

'..... I mean how many times has Matt treated her like that, how many times has he cheated on her then said "I'm sorry babe.... it won't happen again babe!" You weren't really that dumb to think you had a chance?' It looked like she was about to run out of steam but she continued while I got harder.

'What were you thinking? What, that she would be like "Troy I need you... I want you," and then fall into your arms. What about us? What about me? Where you going to sleep with her then screw me over when you both sorted it out?'

Fuck this hurts... How can I be so hard? I thought, she went on;

'Are you ever going to say something, or just sit there...? You know I have known how you felt about her for a while, which made me question how much you loved me if you felt that way about her. Do you even love me and want to be with me now you know that you're never gonna get with Ley?'

'It's not what you think; I like Leyton as a sister (lie) - like my little sister (lie again). That's all and I love you... and she's my best friend's girlfriend. I would never do that to you or even Matt babe.' I think at that point I inhaled deep and prayed she would believe me- my boner was starting to wear off and I hurt a little less.

'So you're trying to tell me that you were not in love with Leyton and didn't want to get with her. Please DO NOT TAKE ME FOR A MUG... I know you and I know you wanted her up until that cruise. What did you finally see how stupid for Matt she is?'

I'm getting harder and she just keeps going on. *Stand up and stroke her hair.... try and kiss her and say sorry?*

*'Look, I had no problems with however you felt as I knew you wouldn't act on it... Fortunately for me you're **"not the cheating type"**, but every time you ran off to her just understand that I had to get my own back. The dog food was nothing compared to all....'*

Hard on lost... *'What you on about... Compared to what? Whit, what did you do?'*

She twitches, inhales- I think this is the first time I have ever seen her act fretful.

'Whitney, what did you do... what are you on about?' What more can she surprise me with; the food seems to bubble in my stomach. I felt sick.

She looks at me, 'What were you expecting, that I would be cool with you mooning over her [Leyton] and not react? I wasn't going to break up with you over that... **I wasn't ready to break up with you yet, so every time you would run to her as her knight...** I would just happen to react in unknown ways!'

She smiles... am a little unsettled. *Really Newton's law of motion is her answer to "teach" me a lesson. Who does that?*

'Your feelings towards Leyton saw you brushing your mouth several times with the toothbrush I used to clean the toilets.... I scrubbed all sorts with it, and then rinsed it with a bit of toothpaste and water so that you would not notice a thing.'

Her smiles widens a crack... she snorts back laughter. I look at her and say, 'Is that when you had all those "cold sores in your mouth?" when you wouldn't kiss me?'

'Am sorry,' was all she managed before she burst into tears of laughter.
I think there is something wrong with me as I should have been real pissed **but** I sat there at the kitchen table, my stomach bubbling and in dumb aware. A normal man would have raised all sorts of stink **but I sat there** listening to her laugh at me: My boner gone and my mouth feeling all sorts of abuse and violation.

She finally gets the laughter underhand, looks at me then goes into another bout of laughter. 'You're taking the f**king piss. What else did you do?' I asked. I was really curious as, if it was that funny then there must have been more and she could be locked up for longer when the police got involved. This was assault by crazy!

'You caused all of this. **You're lucky that I didn't break up with your stupid ass.** I was tempted but thought otherwise. Look, don't worry about what else- just be happy that I still want and love you. That's why I thought we should take this over... why I'm giving you so much "service and attention" and why I made you breakfast. **I think it's time to call a truce.**'

'I wasn't aware we were at war or that I did anything wrong. Whitney what else did you do to "punish" me? ' I was hoping that she would tell me and not act so evasive.

'Don't worry about it now. Let's move on- are you finally over her?' she asked

'Whit, what else did you do?'

'I said not to worry; we are over that lets' move on....' I blacked out for a second- I felt faint. I stood up so sharp I cut myself with the bread knife. I didn't feel the pain but felt the trickle of blood flow from the cut.

I spoke so quietly, 'Whitney what the f**k did you do?'

'If you really want to know, I used your credit cards to pay for all your birthday extravagance.... including Matt's and Leyton's tickets and expenses and our expenses. So your birthday surprise was really on you!' She is smiling sweetly while telling me this, kisses me on the lips and says 'babe I know you're sorry and you have showed me this already, I have come clean and done all this slaving away today to tell you that I forgive you.... I forgive you for all the Leyton shit you polluted our relationship with.'

She kisses the top of my head, 'Whitney!' I could only manage her name.

I thought the Lord's Prayer; **Lord, help me not to commit murder against this crack pot! Deliver me to sound mind so I do not wop some ass. Allow me reasonable thinking before I do something illegal in all States, country and world's to this bitch. Lord, refrain me from such and get her the bleep out of my house.**

'Whit, you for real?' Please God let this woman be joking.

'Well that's what you get for doing me that WAY. Look babe, it's only a little bit of money which you can afford and you did enjoy the trip- didn't you?' She looked at me like I was the one crazy.

'No, it's not just a bit of money as you so put it. It **MY MONEY**- *my f**king credit cards you used.'* Breath, Troy breath, breath - remembers you haven't watched enough *Bones* or CSI to commit the perfect crime and not get caught.

'Forget that for now... how ... **NO,** *why would you...?'* I couldn't finish what I had to say as Whitney cut me off, *'I have* **all** *your credit and debit card details memorized. I've had your details for a long while and frankly I thought you knew. I use it on a regular basis for "feel good shopping trips". Babe it's nothing.'*

First thing to do- **change all my bank cards and online details**. Second **change my damn toothbrushes** and third get her out of my house and life **BUT,** how do you dump crazy without any further retaliation on her part?

The only legal way, *'Whit, um... I love you but there is obviously something wrong with you that you need to get fixed. No normal person does as you have done (what am I on about- I just met a whole host of women that would do the same and more). You need help and am not ready to stick out the treatment you need and will get with you. So I think its best we go our separate ways.'*

It was I like I was speaking to a wall, she smiled widely kissed me on the lip and said- *'babe am not crazy, and am not ready for us to break up as I'm still in love with you; Stop overreacting and come,'* She pulled me to my feet, striped and well you can guess the rest.

We are still together- I don't know why but we are. She rebuffed me breaking up with her, used sex to manipulate me and apologise. I'm a man and sex with Whit is my kryptonite.
I do love her, but I really need to break up with her- I have bought a crouch guard (just in case she gets any ideas in the middle of the night), put child **unfriendly** locks on the cabinets and drawers of the high risk danger items such as knives and forks so I can feel safe, changed and cancelled **ALL** of my credit and debit cards, and found new hiding places for my emergency cash and cards in the house.

I admit that I still want to be with her even after the money and the fact that I paid for my own birthday present (the cruise) for all four of us, including expenses which set me back a cool 5k. **BUT** does staying this Whitney make me a Co-Dependent Dependent if I was to apply the same theory and hypothesis I used on women to men?

My Disclaimer to anyone hurt (mostly the Emotional Dependent females) within the process of this read...

Am guessing your either laughing, foaming at the mouth with anger or well you didn't get that far so you're not reading this: No one was intentionally hurt in the making of this public outcry?? (Or whatever you want to call it). I did make some statements to those I talked to that could be misconstrued as rude and disrespectful- I DO NOT APPLOLOGIZE ABOUT THEM as they were made from an objective point and in the process of a discussion.

To some this may all be bullshit. But it just depends on you and how you reason and interpret things out. These three categories come from years of observations, personal experience, and generally listening and talking (and informal note taking) to many different individuals from different backgrounds and walks of life. Names and any identifying factors of the individuals who participated knowingly and unknowingly in this episode have been changed so that you truly cannot be identified by anyone except if they know you and know your business.

Troy

(If you would like to contact the author please email- Troydefray@gmail.com)

Copyright Defray & Co. Inc

Printed in Great Britain
by Amazon.co.uk, Ltd.,
Marston Gate.